Your Life

Your Guide to Amazing Success and
Incredible Health

Defending Your Life

Your Guide to Amazing Success and Incredible Health

By Dr. Jay M. Goodbinder

LEON SMITH
PUBLISHING

www.LeonSmithPublishing.com

Dedication

This book is dedicated to my wonderful wife and kids who support me and help me feel my purpose every day. Without them, my focus would be less clear, and I wouldn't be able to help as many people.

Acknowledgments

Thanks to my wife, Darcy, and sons, Gabriel and Benjamin, who inspire me to push myself further every day, further than I ever dreamed possible. They taught me how to truly love others and how to feel love.

Thanks to my parents who held steady when I went through rough times. They didn't let me quit on myself.

Thanks to Chad Yonker for our talks on philosophy, metaphysics, life, and just being a great friend.

Thanks to Charlie Webb who taught me the importance of mentors, and who has helped me structure a path to success.

Contents

Introduction

I started writing this book because I wanted to teach people how to keep themselves healthy — how to eat, how to exercise appropriately, and how to have the proper mindset. But this goal turned into something else, something much greater. I wrote this book because I wanted to help people improve their lives. In the past, I placed a lot of pressure and weight on the physiologic part of health. I am a natural healthcare provider, and I worked hard to keep my kids, my wife, and myself — all the people I love — as healthy as possible, by eating right, exercising, and maintaining a positive attitude.

While working, I began to understand that all things are possible, no matter what. It is important to take care of yourself, and it is important to take care of your body. However, I think this book, more than anything, explains why all things are possible and that there's never a reason to fear.

You will always be okay.

Nothing bad is going to happen to you. You are going to make it. You can absolutely achieve your dreams if you want to.

This book is about changing your life. You may start as soon as you finish this book or as soon as you begin reading. Once you've read it, you can't unread the book. You will have knowledge that you never had before, and I expect you will use this knowledge.

In this book, we explore:

- What does it mean to live spiritually in this world?
- What will it take to help achieve all your dreams and goals?
- Why should you never fear anything along the way?
- How does doing your best fit into the achievement puzzle?
- How does saving yourself save everyone else?

I was in a rough, dark place. I struggled. For the majority of my life, I didn't understand my purpose. I was depressed. I wasn't well. I didn't take care of myself. Everything was about *me* and fulfilling all my selfish needs, but I was never happy.

It was like filling up a cup of water that had a hole in the bottom. No matter how much I would fill it up, it would drain back out, and I would be left empty. I wrote this book because I want you to never feel empty again. I want you to know you can achieve anything you've ever wanted to achieve. I wrote this book because I think it will help you understand how to succeed.

I want you to know that you can achieve your dreams and goals without being afraid of failure. The most successful people in the world fail many times before they succeed. Actually, there's no failure at all; there's only failure to try.

I wrote this book because I want to inspire and motivate you, and give you guidelines to help understand that nothing bad will ever happen. Everything is going to work out, and everything is achievable. I wrote this because I want to be lifted up myself. I want you to be lifted up. I want your friends and loved ones to be lifted up. I want my friends and loved ones to be lifted up.

You fulfilling your dreams helps me fulfill mine, and for everyone else to fulfill theirs. My hope is that this book will inspire and motivate you to achieve all your dreams. I wish you the best.

Read the chapters one by one, giving yourself a chance to think about what you read. I cover in-depth, abstract thoughts in this book. I also discuss motivation. If you feel motivated and inspired after you read each chapter, act right away to show you're willing to start working, achieving, and attaining.

The chapters connect to each other, but they stand alone as well. Every time you read a page or chapter or section of the book, think about how it affects you. Apply the information to your life.

Ask yourself: *How is this true in my life?*

When my words make sense to you, act on them immediately. Start doing what you want to do. Life is too short for anything else. Read this book and *act*. Read this book, and think about what you've done. Think about what you've learned. Do not passively read this book. This book should become part of you and help you achieve all your dreams and goals.

The most successful people in the world have mentors and make quick decisions. This book will mentor you as you achieve your goals and also help you make quick decisions.

Start now by thinking about how your life will change and about your next achievement.

I hope that you will:

- Live in eternal bliss
- Gain health and happiness
- Find peace and well-being
- Experience your dreams coming true
- Thank God for every breath
- Never fear again

You deserve to be happy. You deserve to feel good, knowing that you have worked hard for something and achieved it. The way to accomplish that is to work hard so you *can* achieve it, and then feel good about it.

I hope that at the end of every day, you sleep well, knowing that you've done your best. I hope that all your family and friends are proud of you, and they find inspiration in you. I hope you get to see them achieve, feel happy, sleep like a baby, and be inspired by themselves and people around them. I hope that you can help us all be lifted up. It's up to you now. Enjoy!

CHAPTER ONE

Recognizing the Spiritual Self

THE UNIVERSAL SUBCONSCIOUS

People from all over the world use different words for the spiritual *Self* or the *Universal Subconscious*. Different peoples say *God*, *Allah*, or *Hashem*. In whatever religion they practice, persons of faith believe in the universal subconscious or our spiritual self. I point to faith specifically because science argues that spiritual truth doesn't make sense. Science says that only facts are true. Spirituality would be labeled *science* if it was provable, but the fact is that it is *faith*.

Our life experience tells us that something connects us, brings us all together. The word *faith* itself means taking a leap or believing an idea that might not be provable by science; nevertheless you believe it because everything in your being tells you that it is real.

Spirit Goes Through All Things

When I say *spirit*—the *universal subconscious, God*, or whatever you name it—moves through all, I mean that every single entity within our corporeal world, what we see in front of us, is embodied with some level of truth, love, or energy that you may define as a Higher Being. Consider the picture frame in front of you; it was crafted or envisioned by a human being using divine guidance. It is all there in that simple object.

Now the question we have to ask ourselves is whether we are using our divine guidance or using some primitive, more instinctual, worldly need to develop our ideas and projects.

Is this a question of wrong versus right, good versus bad?

As long as you feel strongly that your action is right, in the best interest of the world by helping other people, or at the bare minimum, helping yourself and not hurting anyone else, your intention is driven by divine guidance. The spirit that moves through me realizes my needs and the needs of the world. We are all connected, so if my intention is rooted in love or in birthing a helpful idea, that's great.

Most people see their Higher Being as love and not fear. If you're guided by fear, you are not being guided by love. Therefore, you're not being guided by the spirit that moves through all things; you're not guided by the universal subconscious. You are crawling away from God.

You need to have a clear perception of what *is* actually the truth of the world, versus some indescribable perception created by a blurry lens. Your spiritual self, your soul, needs clarity about the world in order to help yourself, nature, and other human beings when you are making decisions. Then, you can truly help everyone.

I Love Us

I believe that our Higher Being—our God, our energy, our universal subconscious—is comprised of love, not fear. *I love us* expresses our extension into human reality. Obviously, our spiritual self is much greater than what we can see. The world is an eggshell, and we are everything within.

I love us means:

- I understand what the person across from me is saying.

- I understand I need to work through this situation to find a learning moment.

- I understand that whatever others are experiencing, I am experiencing as well.

My ego may not perceive these meanings because I'm struggling within myself. But, anyone who's struggling, who has a problem or disagreement with me, or with whom *you* may butt heads clearly means the best.

I don't think anyone specifically wants to harm the human race. People want to help the whole human race, including themselves. Occasionally, someone acts as our antithesis — or the negative to our positive — when in reality, everyone is trying to do what's best. Good communication with the understanding of truth serves us again so that we can *all* make the right decisions and ensure the achievement of our goals.

If you can simmer down your emotions — some of which are purely your corporeal being — the person that you see in the mirror is the best you. You can see that you are looking at a true representation of your whole self, which includes your spiritual self and your physical self. You can achieve clarity about your *whole* self.

No matter who you encounter or confront, understand that it's not their intention to harm you. Perhaps they're running from fear, and they're scared that you're going to hurt them. Perhaps they can't perceive the truth of the world because they are deluded by an unhealthy physical self. We're all here to find the connection of our corporeal self to our spiritual self. People mean well, unless they really can't see the truth. Perfecting your physical self so that your spiritual self can see through the lens of your body is vital.

God

God is a word that we use to describe everything I've been writing about. Understand that God is true Love, and if we were to live solely within God and the spiritual world, we would not have our egos. We wouldn't be able to see ourselves in the mirror. We wouldn't be able to accept that we are separate people. Rather, we would be part of everything moving through all things, with no judgments of ourselves or anyone else.

If we existed as infinity, as part of the whole, we might be able to perceive things. We wouldn't perceive with our mind, but rather, with our entire energy that connects to everything. We would feel events in the corporeal world, but not understand them. For that understanding, we need our more primitive mind — the brain — that is our system of interpreting the corporeal world.

I love the idea of prayer. I think it's a wonderful thing. I think it's wonderful to understand how truly blessed you are. Every day you can be grateful for what you are being given and take the opportunity to see your spiritual self inside of the corporeal face in the mirror.

Let's say you had a piece of fruit for breakfast. You could say thanks for the meal. Or, you could mourn that you didn't get to eat that fancy breakfast at a fancy restaurant.

If you say thanks for the piece of fruit and understand how useful it is to your body, you will realize:

- You are not starving.
- You have all your faculties.
- You are blessed.

It's amazing to understand that every single day you are blessed with one breath of life after another.

YOU ARE HERE FOR THE GOOD OF YOUR PERSON

You are here for the good of your person. You are the guardian angel of the one you see in the mirror, the animal that you are. Your body has animal instincts. You are trying to survive. That is your body's mechanism. It's primitive, struggling. Your body doesn't reach up to attain higher goals, but your spiritual self, or guardian angel, contains divine guidance. You are trying to take care of this corporeal being. It is a temple to house our divine source.

The Ego

That person you see in the mirror *is* your ego, and it is important. We're all in the world to attain a purpose, and our ego — or the person we see in the mirror, the person who we embody — needs and deserves care.

Your ego has needs:

- To feel important
- To feel like it has a purpose
- To feel pleasure, happiness, and other emotions that human beings feel

In order to achieve, we have to work; that's the hard part. As humans, we'd prefer to sit down and receive whatever we want. We long to click a button and say what we'd like to appear. I worked seven years after my undergraduate education to become a doctor. It would have been easier if after high school I simply said I wanted to be a doctor, and then magically turned into one with all the knowledge I have without the work of school.

That's not the way it is, and there were other driving factors. I wanted to take care of my father, who was born with a heart defect called *hypertrophic cardiomyopathy*. His father died very young of the same heart defect. My father suffered a heart attack on the table when they were trying to put a stent into his heart and ended up with a pacemaker.

I, too, was diagnosed with hypertrophic cardiomyopathy. A cardiologist told me I could never run or do any cardiovascular activity and that I would need beta-blockers for life. I refused to take them. I felt that if I took responsibility and accountability for myself and tried to keep myself as healthy as possible, chances were the genetic code I have wouldn't cause me trouble.

Seven years after I was diagnosed with hypertrophic cardiomyopathy, tests showed no change at all, no progression. I'm managing my condition without medical therapy. I take care of myself and take accountability for myself, for my ego.

The same can be true for you. You may have different genetic predispositions to whatever disease — diabetes, hyperthyroid, autoimmune diseases like colitis, Crohn's disease, and psoriatic arthritis. You need to protect your ego.

I also have psoriatic arthritis. My hand swelled, and I had to go through the medical process of injections. Nothing worked. I had a big, swollen hand and psoriasis from head to toe. It wasn't getting better. I had to take accountability and protect my ego. I did, and now I am on no medication and I am disease free.

Your spiritual self cannot obtain its divine purpose here on Earth unless you take care of your ego as well. That means keeping ego in check; being humble enough to understand that anything you achieve here is because of hard work. You are not given achievement because you deserve it. There's nothing better than hard work. You must cultivate the ability, the foresight, and the drive to work hard to get what you want; there's nothing better. If you are willing to work hard, regardless of outcome, you've achieved greatness whether recognized or not. You're actually training your ego to attain things greater than before you started working.

Your Body Is Like Your Child

You should handle your ego as if it were a child. If you're a parent, you know that you want your kid to be happy, but you also want what's best for your child. I'm a father of two, and I know every day I want my kids to be as happy as possible. But, happiness isn't the end-all and be-all.

I also want them to be and become achievers.

Yeah, I want my kids to be able to go out and play, and I can think: *They're exercising their body, which is wonderful.*

I can also make them happy if I tell them to sit down in front of the TV and watch it all day. They would be happy, but they've been *given* entertainment. They haven't worked for anything, so their bodies become weak and their minds become weak, because they're no longer working for their pleasure. They've been given nothing of lasting value.

Treat your body like a child. Feed your body what it needs. Exercise your body the way it needs. In order for your body to work appropriately, your body also needs spirituality to let it know that it's not alone, it's not by itself, and it actually does have purpose.

Yes, you have carnal needs:

- The need for connection
- The need for love
- The need for intimacy

Meeting those needs is important to your body, and it's important to your spiritual self as well. If you were to let your body tell you to eat fast food every day or to eat all sorts of candy bars, your body's going to be sick. That will inhibit your spiritual self and your ego from fulfilling their purpose.

There is a place for pleasure, but there's also a place for achievement. We'll talk about that later, when we discuss the balance between the two.

The good of your person includes keeping it safe, helping it fulfill its purpose, and helping it be happy. Happiness often comes as delayed gratification. Instant gratification can make you happy in the moment, but delayed gratification can create a longer-lasting happiness.

At all times, you should be thinking: *Is this something that I need to be happy?*

If I create happiness right now, will it decrease my happiness later?

IF IT'S GOOD FOR YOUR PERSON, IT'S GOOD FOR EVERYTHING

When I call the Divine the *universal subconscious*, I mean that we all share it. If you can create positive thoughts and feelings for yourself and for everyone you contact, the entire universal subconscious is steeped in achievement, happiness, and love. You're completely found; you're no longer lost.

Interconnectedness

We are interconnected. As I look across my desk and I see my wife and kids' pictures, I know that we are connected. I can look out into my waiting room and see my patients and know that we are connected, as we are all connected to the universal subconscious. We are one entity; we're just experiencing ourselves through these egos that we see in the mirror.

While you're here for the best interests of your ego, your body, and your purpose, that purpose shouldn't prevent other people from fulfilling theirs. We are all equal entities of a divine being, seeing each other here in the corporeal world.

When you experience dislike or distaste, you are dealing with something within yourself. If you hate someone, you're dealing with the inside of *you*. It's not the other person you hate. Never doubt that when you are upset or hate someone, it's probably something that you hate inside yourself. Work with yourself and let the other person work on their own internal issues.

Arguing whether divine writings account for the actual beginning of time leads to confusion. Now we're using that confusion to incite wars and experience anger and evil when the majority of religious doctrines are about love, connectedness, and *not* fighting. Terrorists kill people on their own soil. People are engaged in wars all over the world. People plan to kill others *in the name of* something. People seem to focus on what is wrong, rather than what is right.

Right now our world contains more right than wrong. We have atrocities happening around the world, but we can't use religion, belief systems, or a person as the reason. The reason lies within *us*.

Gandhi said, "Be the change you wish to see in the world."

I agree with that 100 percent. You have to *be* the change. If you change, then other people will change. There is a person just like you, connected on the other side of this universal subconscious in another ego or corporeal being that will change in a good way, just as you do. When you act with a less than positive intention, keep in mind that you're forcing someone else on the other end of your spiritual plane to deal with a negative intention. The more negativity you bring into our corporeal world, the more difficulty you create to overcome later.

Greatness Leads to Greatness

Greatness leads to greatness, and greatness comes when you focus on positivity. If you use negativity and violence to try to stop others from reaching their goals, you're going to create a negative environment where everyone suffers as if being choked. You can't breathe in this environment, because every breath you have is meant to fulfill a purpose, a goal, or achievement.

To stop someone else from that achievement is horrific. It's spiritual suicide, honestly. You need to be able to connect and understand that what's best for you is also best for me and everyone else. If you are working in such a way that you accomplish what is best for you, then that circumstance, like a ripple effect, can only also have the best outcome for me: when you take care of yourself, when you attain a goal, I benefit as a result. You are not acting selfishly. If you can't see that, if you think what you're doing is the opposite of what's good for me, then you're missing the truth of the world.

I don't believe that anyone is meant to be unhappy or in a state of constant conflict or fear. If you're in fear, you've moved away from the existence of God. God is there, and you should live within that truth and love. If you exist outside of that, you're stepping away from your divine being.

Achievement will lead to achievement. If you can achieve greatness, another person can achieve greatness. This greatness moves through everyone. If you are around it, you will experience it, too. When you feel greatness and achievement, your spiritual self realizes that your corporeal self is capable of achieving greatness. You cease being guided by fear that stops you from attaining your purpose or your god-like self.

If you can push yourself to achieve, even if it's small steps, great things happen. The Great Wall of China takes thousands of steps to travel; you can't traverse it in one step. You take each step individually. Achievement will lead to achievement. The most successful people in the world — whether it's Sergey Brin and Larry Page, creators of Google; or Mark Zuckerberg, founder of Facebook — had to work hard to get where they are, achieving small steps before they achieved their big success.

Any achievement you reach is a great achievement. The next one will be great, too, and the next one. Every day, set a single goal to achieve. When you achieve that, feel good about yourself. The next day, you should set a goal to achieve. It may be completely different, but every day, reach for a different achievement so that you can always feel good about yourself. That is a great present to give to your spiritual self and to your corporeal entity.

Ending the Proliferation of Darkness

Just as achievement breeds achievement, darkness leads to darkness. You proliferate darkness when you've lost your purpose, you feel there's no way out, and you believe you can never be happy with the person in the mirror.

Imagine all of existence traveling through a tube on a single playing field. Every person on that field creates a flare of light behind them. If you create darkness, there will be trails of darkness behind you as well. In that case, you're sharing that with the rest of the universe.

You're giving that darkness to God. You're giving darkness to everything when it was you making the dark choice.

Darkness opposes light. In many religions, our purpose is to bring light to darkness. If you create darkness, other people will create it as well. It's the truth of the universal subconscious. When you bring light into darkness, your god-self becomes apparent here in the corporeal world, unifying us all. Then, we can see that we're all one, not separate beings. We all work for greatness and happiness.

You, for example, can create darkness in many ways:

- Acting with bad intentions
- Not discerning your purpose
- Deciding to lie in bed all day instead of achieving your purpose
- Choosing silence over expressing creative energy

These activities create a vacuum. Other things, other beings, other parts of existence try to make up for that, and the whole world is stretched thin. Our goal is to create depth in our world, in our society, and in our lives as much as possible. The thinner you get — spiritually, not weight- or body-thin — the less purpose you express. Optimally, you could focus on creating light every minute of every day.

When I was a teenager, I ran with a bad crowd. They were basically nice people, but we did a lot of rough stuff: we fought a lot, did a lot of hard drugs, and hurt a lot of people, including ourselves. The deeper I got into this crowd, the worse it got. I found myself no longer friends with people who cared about me. I found myself running away from my family. These good people tried to keep me doing the right things; they practiced an open-door policy. Any time I wanted to come home for dinner, I was welcome. They showed me love, and I couldn't return that love because I was consumed by the darkness around me.

My freshman year of college, I flunked school. I was smart enough to get good grades, but I was so confused that I decided to stop going to class. I didn't need school; I was going to Hollywood to be famous. I was going to be an actor. Well, instead of doing that, I moved in with my parents and worked at Einstein Brothers Bagels. That was fine, however, I wasn't achieving my purpose. I had lost my purpose and was living by my parents' rules.

My father forced me to continue to go to college. He said, "Listen, your mom and I struggled all the time. I didn't go to college, but you are."

He forced me to take one hour a semester at Johnson County Community College, a community college in

Kansas City. He told me I was going to school until I graduated. He cared about me. He was my first mentor.

I went. I didn't like it, but I kept going. I found science and discovered I liked it. I was achieving because I'd been going from class to class, and these achievements started to build on each other. When I found science, I loved it and saw that I could be successful. I took a full load. I ended up with an Associate Degree at Johnson County Community College. Then I went back to the University of Kansas, Lawrence, where I graduated with honors, after having a 0.7 GPA my freshman year. After I graduated, I returned for my doctorate years later and ended up being valedictorian of my doctoral class.

Even though I struggled and flunked, I ended up valedictorian of my doctoral school. Small achievements led to more achievements. Initially, I was on a bad slope. Darkness gave me more darkness, feeding more darkness. I was falling deeper and deeper, separating myself and telling myself I wanted to be alone and didn't want to be around anyone. But once I began achieving I came back. I found my purpose, and now I want to help everyone I possibly can.

CHAPTER TWO

The Physical Being That You're Here to Protect

YOUR PHYSICAL SELF IS IMPORTANT

Your physical self is your child, your animal, and you need to care for it. It establishes how you feel. When your spiritual self enters and experiences the world through your body, you want to perceive the world around you in a positive manner.

Your body cannot project a positive feeling onto your spiritual self if:

- It is sick
- It is starving
- It is choking
- It is struggling to breathe

Your spiritual self feels what your body, your child, is feeling. When your child falls and scrapes their knee, you as a parent feel the pain. In the same way, you feel your body when it is, say, eating fast food. When your body is in a car wreck, you feel the pain. Your body needs to be respected, nourished, and exercised. Your physical self needs to achieve physically as much as your soul needs to achieve spiritually.

You Are Connected to Your Being

You are connected to that being you see in the mirror. It is your ego—that which you are here to protect. The connection is indescribable in that nothing else exists in that manner. You can't remove your body and have your spirit or soul remain here. Your being is the vortex from which your soul explodes through this reality. You two are inseparable. Your soul is connected to every other person within the universal subconscious. In addition, your soul is connected to your being here on Earth, and that is your connection to the corporeal world.

You are connected intimately to your body, similarly to how you are connected to your children, because you are *one*. While you live in this world, your connection with your being, your body, is the most intimate connection you experience.

You Will Feel What Your Being Feels

Your being emanates feelings. It smells and tastes. It feels cold, hot, and pain. Your heart beats faster when you are near someone you love, or when you're about to begin a competition. Your spirit, your soul, also experiences those feelings. Your body is your sensing organism. It's your connection with the entertainment of the world. Whether that entertainment is positive or negative, it is produced by you. The soul feels what your body feels.

The experiences of your body draw a tattoo, or an impression on your soul. You feel an emotion, and it becomes part of your soul for eternity. It doesn't go away.

From the scientific study of epigenetics, we understand that our DNA is basically eternal. Our DNA has existed since the beginning of time. Every experience in the genetic coding of our bodies—and by connection our soul—is now imprinted on the next body and on our children, because our DNA is continuing to travel throughout infinite time.

Your soul exists at a genetic level as you continue to pass through generations. A healing experience will be imprinted on your soul, which will then, like a tributary, pass on to the next generation, which will then affect their bodies and their souls. Again, we are all connected. What happens to your bodies affects you and all eternity from this moment on.

The Body Houses God

Where is this guardian angel I speak of?

When we look in the mirror and see our person, I strongly believe—and many faiths do—that God has an infinite number of angels, meant for specific tasks. They are like the fingers of God, if you will. Your guardian angel is you, and you are here to protect your body.

Have you heard, "Your body is a temple?"

Christians stand in a church and they say, "This is a house of God."

A church and a temple are the same thing; they're analogous to each other. When you put those together, you are saying that your body houses God.

No one knows where a cliché begins. I believe clichés come from a divine place. They come from beyond what we know. We say everyone knows *that*, but where does *that* come from?

The Divine explains the truth to us. The truth is that we should protect our bodies or corporeal selves.

You feel what your body feels, and your body is housing God. You are an angel here, inside of the body that you see in the mirror. You're here to protect it. You are an angel sent forth. You should know that by having a soul, you have Divine Spirit within you.

THE PHYSICAL SELF AS A CHILD

In this world, there's no greater bond than a parent with a child. You want to take care of them. You want them to be successful in life.

You want them to be happy, but there's a balance:

- You want them to be safe, but free.
- You want them to be happy, but successful.
- You want them to be athletic, but intelligent.
- You want them to be good-looking, but humble.
- You want them to be healthy, but happy.

There's a balance to parenting, and that's why I talk about our bodies as our *children*. The physical self as a child is how you should be looking at your body, and how you should be taking care of it.

Mother Knows Best

Imagine your soul as a mother. Many people think of God as a masculine form, and that's fine. Everyone has the ability to visualize a greater being or divine source as they wish. But when I say, "Mother knows best," I see God as a mothering character, trying to take care of her child.

If your body is your child, well, Mother knows best.

I want my children to be incredibly happy, and my wife takes care of them and tries to keep them safe. I'm more the adventurer; I want to step out and experience excitement. My wife tries to build a safe nest. If I follow everything my wife says and my children do exactly as she says, everyone's going to be safe and live a long, healthy life. Mother knows best.

However, my wife also wants my kids to experience all that there is in life while keeping them protected. That's why, again, you need to see your body as a child. Then, you will take care of yourself, just as you would care for your children. You will make sure you are safe; you're not going to put yourself in harm's way.

Keep your body healthy by pushing the limits a little bit. Think of your soul as a mother protecting your body. If you know an action or choice will bring you pain but you do it anyway, you didn't listen to Mother.

You already know what is safe, appropriate, and right, and your body may not want to do that. You may not want to get up early and go to the gym and work out, because even though you know it's best for you, you tell yourself you'd rather sleep. But Mother did know best. It was your body—the baby—that took over and talked you into sleeping longer.

Your Child Has Its Own Will

Mother knows best, but your child has a will of its own. Your body does not want to push itself. It's going to fight you every bit of the way, until you develop good discipline.

You have to be a consistent parent with your children and tell them they don't have a choice by saying:

- Whether you want to or not, you're going to school today.

- Whether you want to or not, you're going to do your homework.

- Whether you want to or not, you're going to practice your instrument, sport, or craft.

Your body has its own will, and if you allow your body to do whatever it wants, it will say:

- I should go out and do drugs.
- I should go out drinking.
- I should go sleep around.
- I should seek instant gratification.

The childlike thing to do is to use the excuse that all your friends are doing it, even though your mind knows it isn't right.

The question is, are you willing to listen to the voice of God, which is you trying to protect your child?

When I was a teenager, I stopped listening to my angel. I stopped listening to what was right, and I started chasing the easiest way to have fun. I lost faith in my understanding of what was best. I lost confidence in my soul.

If you're not confident, you won't listen to what you know to be right. You'll follow the crowd. You'll fall away. You'll pine away and fall victim to what isn't light. You'll fall victim to the darkness.

What is darkness?

Darkness is instant gratification with no vision toward achievement, success, or long-term happiness.

It is a voice inviting you:

- To drink
- To take drugs
- To be promiscuous
- To forget about your friends
- To do whatever is flashy and new

Listen to your intuition, and to what you believe to be right. Go forward with what your body needs rather than what it wants.

KEEPING THE BALANCE BETWEEN ACHIEVE-MENT AND HAPPINESS

We need to keep the balance between achievement and happiness because at all points in time we want to be happy and do what we like. Even if we're doing exactly what we want to do right now, that happiness does not guarantee we're ever going to achieve what we want in the future.

If I want to go to the movies right now, instead of studying for my patients—my patients expect me to learn everything I can about their biochemistry and physiology—I'm failing them. If they come back in and say they are still sick, I'll have no happiness.

You can push off happiness by instant gratification and look towards the future by saying:

- If I study, I can better help my patients.

- If I work hard now, I can be the best football player in the world.

- If I practice guitar right now, even though I'm not having fun because I'm not very good, I *will* be good in the future and have that happiness for life.

That's an achievement. There is a balance.

Happiness Is Temporary

Happiness is temporary. As a baby, all you wanted was to be happy. Babies are more primitive, and that is all they can want. They want sugar. Watch a baby's eyes light up when they have sugar.

They think: *Oh, sugar tastes good!*

Sugar feels happy, and it feels good, but if you keep feeding it to a young child, they may end up with:

- Asthma
- Rheumatoid arthritis
- Colitis
- Crohn's disease

Sugar is not feeding their body. Sugar is feeding their happiness now, but it's not helping them achieve anything. It's not helping them achieve health; it's short-term.

Respect the balance between happiness and achievement. If all you're doing is living for the now, you may feel happy. But that's only temporary, because in the future, you will never have achieved anything.

I have a lot of friends who had more immediate happiness or fun—I'm using happiness and fun together. If you decide to live for now and not work for the future, that's great. Living for now is fine, but you're not leading yourself towards your goals. Your happiness will be temporary; it will not be sustainable. You need to achieve and work for the future sometimes, doing things that you don't want to do in order to succeed at happiness.

Every single day, you have a challenge to meet. If you decide to be happy and have fun and not meet your challenge, you lose that day. If you lose every day, your happiness will be gone. If you can meet challenges and win every single day, you will reach your goals. When you reach your goals, you will have satisfaction and true contentment within life. Happiness will not be temporary; happiness will be eternal.

All Happiness Leads to None

I can be happy today by going to a movie, but then I've spent two or three hours doing nothing that helps me gain or achieve my goals. I go home, and I have nothing to feel excited or happy about except being entertained.

If I want to play video games all day long—winning in John Madden football or some other game like Zelda—I won't achieve anything. I've done that before. In college, I would sit and play John Madden football

all day long. I was obsessed with John Madden football and was so proud of myself because I was great at a video game. I'd play for three hours straight.

Then, I would think: *What did I just do with my life for three hours?*

I literally wasted my life. I didn't achieve anything. There are so many times people will sit and watch TV all day long on the couch. They're not achieving anything.

Then, at the end of the day, how can they ever feel proud of themselves?

How will you ever feel great about yourself—confident, like you're achieving, like you're fulfilling a purpose—if your life is spent on the sofa?

You won't. All you'll be doing is wasting this blessed gift of life in front of you—wasting your existence. It is spiritual suicide to not achieve.

If you go through a day spending a quarter of it not achieving, you're going to lose self-confidence. When you lose self-confidence and start doubting yourself, then you become self-conscious. It's harder to achieve from that point on, because you'll second-guess yourself. Your Divine Will will be confused and muddled.

Achievement Breeds Achievement

If you can train your child-like self in this world to wait for gratification and learn that working toward achievement can bring happiness, you can be happy *while* achieving. When that happens, it's not so hard to get yourself up in the morning and go to the gym before you go to work.

Happiness is a choice. You can thank God you have legs and are able to get out of bed and jog to the gym for exercise. You can be happy to have those legs, and prove it by running. You can be happy you were able to get out of bed and go do something rather than hitting snooze five times because you were too tired. You can be happy you are able to practice guitar for four hours and master your craft. You can learn that your body is in this world to achieve and that happiness can be created with achievement. Then, achievement breeds achievement.

The more you achieve, the more you want to achieve. You break all barriers down, and you realize that anything you want to do in this world, you absolutely can do. It's a matter of working for it. Hard work is integral to achieving your dreams. If you can start working hard now, learning hard work as a trait and a skill, you can achieve more and more every day until it becomes a cycle. It will become who you are.

There's a balance between achievement and happiness, but if you spend a lot more time working on achievement, rather than focusing on happiness, the happiness comes along with the work.

CHAPTER THREE

Sensory Perfection

WHY IS SENSORY PERFECTION IMPORTANT?

Your eyes see your life's playground. You can see what is happening. Your ears hear. Your nose smells. Your mouth can talk and describe things as well as taste. Your hands touch. Your skin feels. These sensations are your gateway into the playground where we all exist. They allow you to see truth. If you can obtain sensory perfection, you can discern the truth of this world.

Making the Correct Decisions

As humans, we're always trying to make the right decisions.

Have you ever asked yourself:

- *Did I do the right thing?*
- *Did I follow the right path?*
- *Is this my soul mate?*
- *Is this who I'm supposed to be married to for life?*
- *Is it bad that my friends don't want to spend time with me more?*
- *What am I doing wrong?*

You ask yourself these questions because you are confused. You don't trust your decisions. Maybe you haven't achieved sensory perfection, that ability to see the truth. Once you get to a point in time where you can trust your senses and the portal from which your soul can see into this world, you experience less doubt and regret. You know that every day you're making the right decisions.

Without sensory perfection, you can't make the correct decisions. A blurry lens, a medium that no longer allows you to see the truth of this world, will cause you to make incorrect decisions.

The Union Between Will and Purpose

If you can attain sensory perfection—if you can see the truth of the world—it's much easier to understand your purpose. Your purpose in this world is to help raise everything up, to bring light into the darkness, to bring happiness and a feeling of purpose to everyone else. The union between will and purpose begins when you see that your will is the child, or the body. Your child sometimes wants things that you don't want to give it, because you don't think it best. When you perfect your sensory perception—your understanding of your surroundings, environment, and the truth of this world—then the will of your child can match your purpose.

A marriage between your will and your purpose is a blissful event which occurs when your will recognizes:

- *It feels great when you are driven and can help achieve your goal.*
- *True happiness is sustainable happiness.*
- *What is good for others and what's good for you are the same.*

When your will wants to achieve wonderful things, you are free to act every day, no longer questioning what you're doing. When married to your purpose, your will never pulls you to eat that bad meal or to act against your purpose or path. When your will matches your purpose, your energy and focus align to achieve that purpose. When that happens, the whole world is better.

Perfect Confidence

Confidence is vital. So many people are self-conscious, worrying about social media and the judgment that others place on them. In addition to worrying about judgment about themselves, they've begun to judge other people.

When you obtain sensory perfection, and unite your will with your purpose, you don't ever have to doubt yourself again. Your understanding of this world's truth is crystal clear. You can leave doubt behind because your perception of the world is correct. Your purpose is clear, and your guardian angel—your soul—can understand what's happening in the world, and make the correct decisions.

You may wonder if you are being a good parent to your child. You may let them have fast food or do questionable things because they want to.

Is that going to be healthy for the child?

Probably not. When you give in to what a child wants, even though you doubt the decision, you are not perfectly confident.

If information is coming to you through a clear lens—meaning your body is in a state of sensory perfection—you will never doubt yourself again. You will never second-guess your decisions.

You will know:

- The friends you have are the ones that you should have.
- The spouse you're choosing is the right one.
- The house you want as a home for you and your family is the best for all of you.
- The state you've chosen to live in is the right state.

The decision you make to help somebody — or not — will be the right decision. You never will second-guess yourself, or deal with self-consciousness. You can always be 100 percent sure and 100 percent fine with every decision you make. You will cease to have any anger or depression.

UNDERSTANDING THE CORPOREAL WORLD

From birth, we try to understand why we're here and where we came from.

The question *what are we doing here?* creates fear within us. As babies we are thrust into this world of chaos, not knowing what to do.

Everything is blurry at that point, but you grow to understand the corporeal world as a place that will:

- Further your purpose
- Help your spirit grow
- Help other people's spirits grow
- Help you connect
- See your spiritual self within your flesh
- See the universal subconscious in other people

Looking out through your eyes, you realize the person walking by you is just another part of you. Your head is seeing its tail for the first time and it is a wonderful experience. The corporeal world is the place where everything connects. It's important to understand what you're actually doing here.

Living Truth

Through your corporeal experience, your soul perceives this world. You were first a spiritual entity that's part of everything but unaware of its own existence. Now you are a corporeal being who's aware of its existence, but less aware of the fact that it's connected to everything.

When you realize that we are all connected, that we're all here for good, and that nothing bad is going to happen, it takes a lot of stress from you. Everything will work out, and circumstances will be as they will be. You can stop worrying and start making decisions guided by love instead of fear.

A natural process occurs. You lose things, and it hurts you. In pain, you are not seeing the truth in front of you — that we're all connected and we're all one thing. This blurry lens into this world doesn't allow you to see that truth. Therefore pain happens, and then it creates pain for everyone — pain for those involved and pain for those who witness it. A lack of trust spreads within the truth of this world.

Divine Guidance

How do you clean the blurry lens?

Sensory perfection makes your body aware of everything in your environment so that the truth will always be clear. Your divinity aligns itself through perceptive perfection. Your soul is the tributary of a divine being, and you are the angel that takes care of your body. If you can clearly understand the truth of this world and make decisions, you are using divine guidance.

You can help create unity and a wonderful world to live in—a playground. You should live in a place of happiness, and in this place you should enjoy your ego, your person on this plane. The more you can use your divine guidance rather than a blurred existence, the more that you can enjoy your time here.

Roadmap to Ascension

The roadmap to ascension involves cleaning up your physical self, understanding why you're doing it, then using divine guidance to achieve. This roadmap makes the whole world easier and a playground for eternity.

This morning I woke up at 5:15—like I do every day—and worked out. When I'm done working out, I know I am going to feel great. Some mornings I'm less than clear, but I see things in a positive manner, so I push myself to do it. I am not cynical or weighed down. I know from experience that if I don't work out in the morning I feel like I'm pushing through my day because I'm always tired. If I didn't work out I'd be trying to make it through, and then I'm not living; I'm surviving.

If I've worked out in the morning and eaten a healthy breakfast—not a bunch of waffles and pancakes—I feel great inside and can't stop it. A world of emotion bubbles over; I feel like I want to help everyone and myself, and I'm excited to talk to people and be a part of their day. Without those healthy choices, I'm tired and don't want to connect. I want to stay by myself, be in my head, or go surf the Internet and be away from people.

The roadmap to ascension involves perfecting everything so that when you wake up in the morning, you know that you're truly in a heavenly place. There's no danger, you can achieve whatever you want, and you're here for a purpose. You perfect your being in this world, and understand that you are divinely guided to help everybody achieve their purpose, including yourself.

If I'm working out, eating healthy, maintaining a positive attitude, and fully understand that I'm here for the best of everyone including myself, my world becomes a heavenly existence. If everyone else does it, too, this path *is* a roadmap to ascension for our entire existence.

THE PLAYGROUND FOR ETERNITY

This world is the playground for eternity. We can choose to make this a beautiful playground, or choose to make this playground a place to avoid. Life here should be wonderful and purposeful.

Every day you should:

- Feel you have a place and purpose
- Feel safe
- Feel you can laugh and have fun
- Feel wonderful

But as it is now, this playground of ours is ripe with scary realities. The Internet is a cesspool. Many people use it as a productive tool, but if you spend too much time on the Internet, it's easy to be pulled into a questionable place where you can be seduced into forgetting yourself. If everything on the Internet existed here on Earth, it would be horrible for all of us. This plane should be a playground, and you should see it as a playground for eternity, and begin to enjoy life.

Optimizing Existence

Optimizing existence is expressed by connecting with the rest of *you*. When you see a person struggling, don't just go along your way and retreat inside your head. Connect.

Let's say you see an older person who doesn't bend well, and they drop their cane. Go pick it up and consider how you feel inside. I know every time I've done something similar — picking up something and handing it to a person — I've thought about it afterwards, and it felt good.

Let's say you're finished eating, and you're going to put your leftover food in the trash. Then, you see a homeless person sitting there, hand it to them, and ask if they would like some food to eat. It's no big deal for you; you were going to throw it away anyway.

Do it, and guess what?

You're going to feel good.

Why not feel good all the time?

Actions like these bring spiritual cleansing and great feelings. You practice them and they become habit, and transform who you are. You will feel good all the time.

Who tells you to feel bad about feeling good all the time?

Feel good all you want. Take the steps to do it.

You can decide to either optimize existence and create betterment, or you can make decisions that won't do so. First, you must know what the correct decisions are. Your lens needs to be clear; your body needs to be optimal; your days need to start off right. Once your whole intent is to do things that feel great, good things are going to happen. You can make that decision.

The World Is All We Have

This world that we live in—this playground, if you will—is all we have within the physical realm. If you don't like it here, your only other choice is to not exist at all. By not exist, I don't mean *die*. I mean to exist, but not consciously. I mean to be part of the world without a feeling mind. You've chosen to be here with an ego, with the ability to see yourself as a person. Every breath within the corporeal world is a blessing and a gift. Every single morning when you wake up and take one breath, you receive a gift. It is a heavenly gift that you are here and able to explore yourself and your purpose.

All you have *here* is all you have. Respect it all; respect the environment we share. I think we all feel this need in our soul. Children are concrete in their thinking, but as we get older, we change. When I see a worm slithering on the ground, I'm not going to stomp on it. I don't seek to hurt things. I don't look at a dog who's barking and then kick the dog. That doesn't make sense.

You're here to improve things. You're here to make things better, and I think you realize that when you dig down to the root of the matter.

You don't see a lady walking out into a parking lot and think: *Wow, I hope she slips and falls. That will make me happy.*

No, it won't make you happy. You shouldn't wish pain on others because you are dealing with pain. This is all you have *here*, and I think you should make the best of it.

The Subconscious Will Fold In on the Conscious

We are connected to a universal subconscious. Once we realize that we're all connected, it becomes easy to bring divine guidance into the corporeal world. There are so many religions and belief systems that tell us to bring goodness, happiness, and light to the darkness.

I think all religions have one thing in common. They refer to the *end of times*, the arrival of a figure, or the resurrection of a vital person. This commonality is the universal subconscious folding in on the conscious.

This event is much bigger than our physical world. This is a complete connection between all things in the spiritual world *and* the physical world. The subconscious will fold in on itself, time as we know it will end, and heaven will begin for everyone, forever.

As I shared earlier, I was once in a really bad place, a dark place. I took pride in thinking that I was a bad person, pride in the idea that I could control others. I was *not* happy, and I could never find someone who would truly love me. I was taking pride in doing things that I knew weren't me, simply to attract attention. I was in a sad place, wanting attention and experiencing depression. Then I realized that my friends were going away, I was no longer seeking love, and I wasn't loving life. I needed a change.

Honestly, my most important choice was deciding to get my body healthy. That decision entailed exercising, finding the appropriate foods to eat, and eating them consciously, knowing that I was improving my body. This way, I allowed myself to reach a higher purpose. Getting your body healthy is your first step as well. Then, everything else will become clear—defining your purpose, finding your will.

I used to go to the gym four hours a day, to work on one body part, four days a week. I was sore all the time. I grew a lot of muscle, and I'm not even sure if that was the right way to go about things. In fact, I'm pretty confident it *wasn't*. I was breaking down my joints. But I was putting my focus into improving my body, rather than breaking it down. Shortly thereafter, not only was I working out well, but I was also eating cleanly.

Then I asked myself: *What is my purpose?*

This happened long before I became a doctor, before I ever knew I was *going* to. I didn't think it was possible for me to be a doctor. I only knew I wanted to do something.

I went back to college and made some good decisions for my future. However, I was still living under the assumption that I had limits. I was limited by what I could achieve. I graduated with my undergraduate degree, a Bachelor of Science in Community Health. I knew I liked health, and I wanted to teach about it, but teaching wasn't enough. I had a limited amount of knowledge, and I wanted more. But, I thought this degree was all I could do.

I tried to place myself into work that appeased my brother, the businessperson. He told me to work for a corporation and get myself a *good* job. That's what I did. In that workplace, I began to think I had no reason to be awake. I had no reason to live. I wasn't fulfilling any purpose. I was there to earn the paycheck, and achieve superficial goals of buying a car and nice clothes. I was committing spiritual suicide. I started going to bed at seven o'clock each night because I had no reason to be awake anymore.

I was writing memos in the middle of the night. I'd wake up at three in the morning and write how people should be eating—proper nutrition—while working at an IT corporation. I would take my memos into work and tell people how they should be eating and hand them out. I finally said I wanted to be a doctor, to use my scientific knowledge. I wanted to be able to *be* a doctor and truly understand health.

I decided to seek my doctoral degree, which was ultra-important to me. Many of my co-workers asked why I was I quitting a job where I would always make good money. They told me I didn't know what I was doing, that I couldn't quit a guaranteed position.

I told them I didn't want to live anymore, that every single day I wished I wasn't alive. I wanted to die as fast as possible, because I had no reason to live while doing that job. I had no purpose. I didn't care if I made *any* money, as long as I could fulfill my purpose. I told them I was unhappy, and I knew I would be happy if I went back to school.

Of course my brother, the consummate businessperson, agreed with all of my co-workers. He told me I was stupid and accused me of not wanting to work. I told him I wanted to do something that I believed in, something that I could feel. Even my boss had said he thought my corporate job wasn't the career for me as I was writing memos about nutrition instead of rollout strategies on how to improve the business.

I laughed with him for a second, but I left. I had questioned myself multiple times, especially when I started the doctoral program, which was super intense. I had never studied like that. But I'll tell you, the first day of my doctoral program, I walked into the advisor's office, and I told him I planned on being valedictorian of my class.

He said, "That's a good goal."

But four years later, I *was* the valedictorian of my class. I gave a speech at graduation. It was my purpose.

I found my purpose, but it all started with improving my physical self. I had to get my physical self in check before I could even look through the lens to discover my purpose. You must clear your lens. Clear your body. Take control of your child, otherwise your child will rule the roost.

If you let a child do whatever they want, they're going to eat candy all day, and not be a happy person. If you can take control of your child, taking care and control of your body, perfecting that, everything else follows.

You can make the right decisions and end up exactly where you want to be. Right now, I'm *exactly* where I want to be. Every day I wake up like a lion, jump out of bed, and serve my purpose.

You can do the same thing.

It was a long journey for me. I tried to work out and eat right, but I didn't always know how to do either. Find a mentor—someone who wasn't healthy, who wasn't happy—and who is now happy, healthy, and successful with great relationships. Ask them how they did it. Chances are, they took care of their body first. They achieved sensory perfection, and then slowly they attained what they wanted.

Once I started working on my health, it took ten years before I hit a point where I thought: *Wow, I really love my life!*

The journey was a ladder. I started on the first rung, and kept going up, up, up, until I arrived here. It's still a journey. Every day, I'm trying to fulfill my purpose. It all started with accomplishing sensory perfection.

CHAPTER FOUR

The Lens to See the Truth of the Corporeal World

SHARPENING YOUR SENSES

Think about sharpening your senses as you would sharpen a razor. A very sharp razor will cut your hair extremely close and smooth. There are no cuts, no scratches; there's no pain. Everything is clear, and you look beautiful and fantastic. Now, if you have a dull razor; old, rusty, and unkempt; you are going to pull your hair, causing pain and irritation. You may even cut yourself. Essentially, you will become irritated and inflamed, and in the end you are not going to get the results that you want.

Likewise, you need to sharpen your senses in order to obtain exactly what you want. Your senses are the way that you connect to what's around you. They are the way to perceive this world in its truest form. Your senses are the way you connect, whether through touch, smell, taste, sight, or hearing; all these senses are the way you recognize and connect to our world. The sharper your senses, the better your spiritual self can recognize the world around you. Work to optimize all these systems and everything that is contained within them.

To sharpen your senses, you need to understand what they do, or at least in a broad scope, know how to sharpen them. You need to know the exact steps to take, and where to begin. Maybe you want do the things I've suggested, but are waiting for me to give you direction. I understand that, so here's where we're going to start, with a little bit of an overview of what you can do *now* — right now, starting today — to sharpen your senses and focus your lens into the corporeal world clearly.

THREE WAYS TO FOCUS YOUR LENS

Optimizing Sugar Intake

Sugar ingestion throws off hormones in your body. This imbalance causes difficulty in processing the information you receive on a daily basis. When you have a glass full of orange juice you might think it is a healthy choice because it contains a lot of vitamin C. This may be true, but when you drink a glass of orange juice, it has as much or more sugar than a glass of soda pop.

It doesn't matter whether you ingest sugar as refined sugar or natural sugar in fruit, honey, agave, or whatever form; you are still ingesting sugar. Sugar is sugar, no matter how you calculate it. When you ingest sugar, your blood sugar levels spike and in return, your body produces insulin to bring those blood sugar levels down.

A couple of things can happen at that point. One, the insulin begins to damage a part of your brain called the *hippocampus*, which is responsible for controlling your sleep-wake cycle. As a result, your sleep might be poorer, and your energy during the day will likely drop. Second, the hippocampus is responsible for short-term memory, so you may notice brain fog or memory problems.

If you want to focus on optimal glucose use, your hippocampus must be functioning properly. You do not want your blood sugar to spike because it will begin to create high insulin levels, which increase the chances that you are going to create and store fat. When you create and store fat in your body, your body begins to make more estrogen, and you are more likely to experience estrogen-related issues such as polycystic ovarian syndrome, breast cancer, and thyroid cancer.

A sure way to avoid this is by eating multiple small meals a day. You should also consider your daily portions of fruits, vegetables, nuts, seeds, and meats.

Think of your food intake in these terms:

- 50 percent vegetables
- 25 percent meats
- 25 percent fruits, nuts, and seeds

You might consider quinoa every now and then because it is a high-protein seed. This is what your daily values should look like. If you follow this guideline, you will be able to control your blood sugar in a safer and more efficient manner.

Optimizing Stress Responses

The notion that stress is a bad thing is incorrect. You experience stress, and you can also experience *distress*. Sometimes stress can motivate you to move. It can propel you forward in life to achieve anything you want. Distress on the other hand—which is what I think pervades our society these days—is a constant, underlying feeling of anxiety.

Distress can be generated by many different factors:

- Deadlines at work
- Driving in traffic
- An empty gas tank
- A political debate
- Events happening halfway across the world
- Distractions on the Internet
- Phones ringing all day

I would beg you to try to separate yourself from your technology for a little while. That can and will help.

Another way to help minimize the distress in your life is to meditate in any manner or form. Sit down and give yourself twenty minutes every day. Have a cup of tea, put your phone away, turn the TV or radio off, and focus on yourself and well-being. Just sit on the couch, or sit outside and look at nature. Tune everything and everyone out and relax your mind and your body. Meditating will improve the way you respond to stress.

Another step to help relieve the stress you are experiencing is to make gratitude statements every day. Before you go to bed tonight, think of five to ten things you are truly proud to say about yourself. Say them out loud or write them down on paper.

Some examples might be:

- You have a roof over your head.
- You know where your next meal will come from, so you will not starve tonight.
- You have all your faculties.
- You have friends and family that love you.

You can gaze in the mirror and know there's somebody in the world right now that would look at your life and consider it heaven. They would give their entire life just to be you for one day.

You will soon realize that happiness is a choice. Only you can choose to be happy.

Gratitude will change the way you respond to stress. A sandwich to a starving person is an amazing thing. For most of us, if we have a sandwich in front of us we can see the true beauty of that sandwich. For others, they might say they will eat half of it and throw the other half away. They are showing they do not understand the true beauty of being nourished. Your perspective matters.

If you are stressed everywhere, obviously you are going to have a short temper. You may not see things clearly, and you may get angry with people that you love. You may act out for ridiculous reasons because you cannot handle even small problems. If your cup's full and you put a little more water in it, it's going to spill over. If you can pull some of the water out of the cup, and then put a little bit of water back in, it's no big deal. It's the same with stress. If you can control the levels of stress, then adding a little bit extra when something random occurs should be no big deal.

Getting Rid of Toxins

Do you think that there are many synthetic chemicals in our environment?

There absolutely are. Some sources report that there are around seventy-seven *billion* tons of synthetic chemicals put into our environment on a yearly basis.

Your liver detoxifies your body, and it produces neurotransmitters that process or *deaminate* your proteins into the amino acids needed for body processes. If your liver is toxic, your body can't function correctly, which means you can't think clearly. You can't perceive clearly.

A lot of these toxins are called xenoestrogens, which create extra estrogen flow in your body, increasing its likelihood to store fat. Also, extra estrogen makes you more likely to develop estrogen dominant issues such as uterine fibroids, endometriosis, and polycystic ovarian syndrome.

More men are developing hypothyroidism, a condition previously found primarily in women. Men are also accruing xenoestrogens, resulting in high levels of thyroxine binding globulin and interfering with thyroid function. Most doctors do not typically test these levels. Getting rid of toxins will help tremendously.

You can detoxify several ways:

- Drink a lot of water every day: distilled, reverse osmosis, or ionized.

- Keep your food clean; wash produce to remove chemicals.

- Eat meat that is 100 percent grass-fed, organic.

- Make sure chicken meat and eggs are from pasture-raised birds.

- Buy local, organic fruits and vegetables.

- Eliminate Splenda, Equal, and saccharin.

Artificial sweeteners taste sweet but they don't do anything good for you. If you can do those things — eat the right foods, keep the toxins out, detoxify yourself on a consistent basis — your body is going to be a whole lot healthier, and a much better vessel through which your soul may see the corporeal world.

To sharpen your senses, you need to take care of yourself. No doctor is ever going to cure you; not I, nor any other doctor. No one else is going to cure you; not a friend, not a family member. In the end, it will be up to you to take care of yourself. If you can't take care of yourself, no one else can.

Remember:

- Eat right
- Manage your stress
- Exercise
- Maintain a positive attitude

- Keep toxins out
- Limit your sugar

If you follow these guidelines, your senses will be crystal-clear sharp.

That's just the way it is. You become a better person when you are willing to work hard to achieve goals, better than the person who was given everything. Congratulations to you for being given that *opportunity* to work harder. Congratulations!

ACHIEVING YOUR GOALS

Achieving your goals is vital. Your goal should be to achieve whatever makes you content; to achieve whatever makes you happy. But achievement is not given to you. It's called an achievement because you worked for it.

As human beings, every single one of us should be focused on achieving goals. We should have goals, not just sit there and look around and tell ourselves we are getting through this life so we can die.

No! You're here for a purpose. You should have goals, and achieving them should be paramount every day. You should have short-term and long-term goals. Your goal today should help you achieve your long-term goal tomorrow.

The Goals Become Clear

You must sharpen your senses. You must improve your body. You must eat right and exercise. Do everything necessary to optimize yourself. Once you really clean yourself, take away the stress, do more meditation, and visualize what would make you feel your purpose in life, your goals become clearer.

My goal is to always have a happy and healthy family. My goal is to be the best doctor I can be and help every single person that comes into my office. Every single day I'm learning how. Your goals could be completely different, and that's great. In order for your goals to become clear, you have to take care of yourself first. *Then* they become clear.

Don't tell yourself that you're going to do this the rest of your life when you're an unhealthy person who doesn't know what they want. You might end up on a path you don't want. That's how people end up living an incongruent life—a pretty terrible thing. I would recommend taking care of yourself before you make any long-term goals.

The Path Becomes Clear

Once you've made the decision to change your life, do those things to keep your body clean and optimal, and the goal becomes clear, the path becomes clear. If you are 100 percent certain of your purpose and know what specific goal to create, the path to those goals becomes clear. You will know what steps you need to achieve that goal.

Let's say you want to make the high school football team, or become a cheerleader in college. There are certain steps that everyone must take to achieve those goals. If you want to be a high school cheerleader, you've got to have good balance. Maybe you need to learn gymnastics. You work on every single one of those things every day. Spend thirty minutes or an hour practicing. That's your path.

If you want to make the high school football team, you need to be strong. You need to be fast. Run as fast as you can every single day, because running fast helps you run faster. If you want to learn the game, study the playbook and the theme of your coach's strategy. If you want to play a specific position, determine what your body needs to do and where your mind needs to be, and work on those things every day.

If you want to be the best chef in the world, cook every day, create recipes, and work on developing your palate. Understand the different cooking methods, and consider going to culinary school.

School is a great tool in achieving whatever you want; it's not necessary, though. And if you're really driven, school can actually slow you down. If your purpose is to be an entrepreneur and save the world with an eco-friendly innovation, the science is there, and you can read the book. If you've seen the movie, *Good Will Hunting*, the young man reads books in the library and knows more than people in school. You can spend time studying what you love by yourself, instead of being forced to go through a curriculum where you're learning things that you may not love. Follow what you love, follow your path, and you'll achieve your goals.

Walking the Path Becomes Simple

After you recognize the path, it may appear difficult. If you want to play the guitar, starting can be tedious. You won't be the best guitar player in the world by playing for an entire year. But if you can spend a half hour every day for a whole year playing the guitar, you will have your favorite songs learned. You can sing them and playing becomes fun. Then, you're not practicing; you're *playing* the guitar. The path to your goal of being an accomplished guitarist becomes simple, because you're enjoying it.

Playing guitar for half an hour a day and within a year, playing the guitar will be as fun as seeing a movie. It's relaxing, something that helps you forget about some of the stressors outside; forget about anxiety; get away from the computer, phone, and TV; and have your family singing around you. If your kids, a year from now, sing while you play the guitar, imagine the satisfaction you will gain by being able to do that. I can imagine going camping with my boys—which would be amazing—and playing guitar, sitting there, and singing a song in nature. It's a beautiful thing.

Whatever your goal, practice every single day and make that your commitment. Every day, you will take a step toward greatness. At some point in time, that path becomes fun. It stops being tedious. Instead of climbing up the ladder, it's going down the slide. You've achieved to the point where everything you do can be a heavenly experience.

You can do it. You can achieve everything you've ever wanted; you need to make a choice.

So many people say they want one thing, but want something more:

- To hang out with their friends
- To go to bed early
- To sleep in
- To drink a soda pop
- To do drugs, drink, or smoke cigarettes

If you truly want your goals and are single-minded in focus to achieve it, you can achieve anything.

CHAPTER FIVE

Achieving a Perfect Sensory Self

GIVING THE BODY WHAT IT NEEDS

Give your body what it needs to optimize and make you feel good, as well as give yourself a base for all the achievements that you plan to accomplish. If you can give your body what it needs, it will work smoothly like a well-oiled machine. Then, whatever purpose you are working towards is easier to attain and your work is more efficient. If you can give your body what it needs, whatever you want is attainable.

Immediate Gratification

What are you going to do today that is going to satisfy you, to make you happy, and to work as a step towards the next evolution of your life?

Today, we all want to do certain things that are going to make us feel good, but those things can detract us from what is in the future, the long-term goals we have. If we can give ourselves something today—a nice little carrot to chew on to get us over the hump—things will work out a lot better.

Let's say again that you want to learn how to play guitar. Now if you just sit there, and play note after note after note—no songs involved, just note after note—you'll become bored and never achieve your goal. You want to be good at guitar and able to play songs. Give yourself tasks to work on—playing notes, working on finger positions—but also make it fun. Try to play one of your favorite songs for a bit so that you can have fun and hear what you want. Yet, you're still working for a future goal.

The same process applies when feeding your body.

You want:

- To eat healthy foods
- To optimize all parts of your body
- To decrease inflammation
- To enjoy proper organ function
- To work productively
- To think clearly

When you're eating healthy, make your food taste good. When you work out, try playing a competitive sport instead of lifting weights or running all the time; try different activities to keep you going and enjoying your workout. Avoid the monotony of: *lift a weight and put it down, lift a weight and put it down.* Give yourself more fun, in which case, you're receiving immediate gratification, as well as working on long-term satisfaction.

Long-Term Satisfaction

Your body is a tool for achieving your dreams and goals. Condition it by giving it what it needs.

To optimize, your body needs you:

- To work out
- To take time off
- To rest
- To manage inflammation
- To eat healthy proteins
- To eat healthy fatty acids (omega-3s and omega-6s)
- To limit sugars
- To eat multiple times a day
- To drink clean water

Spend the majority of every day working toward achievement and remember to give yourself a little bit of fun. If you are consistent over the long-term, the results build and build and build to a point where working toward long-term goals and dreams that you have becomes fun.

You get better and better and better, like a ladder spiraling toward heaven. Your body moves into a better condition. It becomes easier to do the things you've always wanted to do. Your daily, immediate gratification leads to the long-term satisfaction of knowing that you're capable of everything. There's nothing that will ever stand in your way, because you've built up this amazing confidence in your body's ability. You never have to doubt your body because you give it everything it needs.

Clean water, good food, good sleep, good exercise, good rest: all these things are so important. If you can fulfill these needs, your ability to achieve your dreams and goals and attain your purpose—and make that purpose not so difficult that it exhausts you—it is right in front of you.

Warmth in Our Corporeal Environment

When you think of love, you think of warmth. Imagine your mother or father holding you. Imagine embracing your spouse or your kids in true love. You don't think of cold. Love is a warm environment with the sun shining down, greenery in the leaves of trees.

If you are able to give your body what it needs, it will embrace your soul with warmth as you're standing there. If you're giving your body what it needs, your chances of understanding your purpose and living it are great, no matter what happens. You can always feel that warmth. You will always know you're in the right place. You're not on the outskirts of the universe, walking alone. You're not alone, because you fit within the picture of the world.

Everyone is trying to achieve their purpose. When you achieve your purpose, giving your body what it needs so it reacts the way it's supposed to, you fit within a puzzle of helping everyone else achieve their purpose. The warmth and love that everyone feels for themselves will shine outward. You can feel that as well.

Your corporeal environment will be filled with warmth. It won't feel cold, and it won't feel aggressive. People won't be attacking each other, because they will be confident that they're achieving their purpose. They won't have to tear anyone else down due to their insecurities because you will help lift them up. You will help everyone spiral up to a heavenly existence. Giving your body what it needs today, giving your body what it needs tomorrow and for the infinite future, allows your body to feel warm again.

Your body is the lens to see into our corporeal world. Give it what it needs brings warmth. It will make you feel good every morning. When you wake up, you'll open your eyes and jump out of the bed like a lion, ready to serve your purpose. It's a wonderful feeling, but it also allows you to see clearly into the world.

Giving your body what it needs eliminates self-doubt and gives you self-confidence. When you have self-confidence, share it with other people. You want to explore and not allow fear to guide your life. Love guides your life instead. Please never look past that fact. I believe you will always give your body what it needs.

GIVING THE MIND WHAT IT NEEDS

Your mind has certain needs, just like your body and soul. When you give your mind what it needs, it allows you to relax. When the mind is in an imbalanced state, missing what it needs, you're going to lack memory, lack quickness of thought, or experience a brain fog. Your mind needs two important things to be crisp, clean, and fire appropriately. Those two things are achievement and security.

Achievement

We all rationalize what we're doing in the world. We try to give ourselves some explanation of what we're doing here.

When we talk about achievement, it's great to be able to think: *I was able to achieve this. I am capable of so much more.*

Achievement breeds confidence. Confidence eliminates self-doubt. When you are confident in yourself, it's amazing how much you want to help other people. When you're not confident, you don't care about helping other people. You feel so insecure about yourself that you don't want people to find out that you feel like a failure. Giving yourself achievements helps you feel great, and then you can help everyone feel great.

Let's say I set a goal today. I'm going to make sure that I eat no bread. I'm going to drink no milk. I'm going to ingest no chemicals. Everything I eat is going to be organic. That sounds easy.

What you put in your mouth is an easy thing, right?

Well, it's not. For so many people, their health and confidence has deteriorated and their mind is not working properly because of what they have put into their body. Maybe they put McDonald's into their body, which we know isn't good food. Or they've decided to go out to Dairy Queen and eat a Blizzard. These items don't nourish bodies. If you know these are the wrong things to eat, and yet you do it anyway, you decrease your achievement. You haven't achieved anything, so you decrease your confidence in yourself. You can't feel excited about anything.

If anyone's here to protect yourself, it's you. You are the only guardian angel you have, so it's up to you to make the right decisions. If you've acted otherwise, knowing it's the wrong thing, you're going to lose confidence and a lot of your happiness.

Security

You need to feel secure. A level of security comes with giving yourself achievement and the happiness that comes with it. The root of *security* is *secure*. You want to feel secure in yourself so that you don't question yourself and worry about others are getting to know you. You don't want to be embarrassed of who you are. When you feel secure, you can be proud of who you are. A person who does not feel secure is not going to open up and share their gifts with the world.

If you are not going to share your gifts with the world, you are robbing the world. If you are not opening up, talking to people, and expressing who you are, you're robbing the world of your art. You're robbing the world of who you are and what you have to offer.

The world is void of greatness because systems breed insecurity. Your greatness is so necessary for the happiness of everyone. You create a void when you are insecure. Your mind needs to feel secure in achieving things and fulfilling your purpose. You are not fake. Claim who you are, what you believe in, and climb the ladder to become the best that you can be each day. Then you will feel secure and can help the world feel secure as well.

GIVING THE ANGEL WHAT IT NEEDS

The angel is you. You are here for a purpose. Inside yourself lives an angel who moves your body and guides you. When you give the angel what it needs, you are giving God what It — He or She — needs. Giving your angel what it needs and giving everyone else's angel what they need are the same.

When you help every other angel fulfill their purpose, you:

- Ascend
- Help eliminate fears
- Understand that we are all here for good
- Recognize that love is everywhere

Your goal is to feel secure, help everyone achieve, and eliminate your self-doubt.

Understanding That We Are All Here for Good

When you woke up this morning, you didn't wake up thinking that you wanted to hurt people, to ruin lives, to do bad things, destroy the environment, or create war. That wasn't what you thought when you woke up this morning. What you woke up thinking with was one of two things.

Maybe you woke up and thought: *I'm excited about the day! I get to go achieve something!*

On the other hand, maybe you thought: *I don't know why I'm here, and I wish I could just lie in bed all day. I don't want to get up because I hate my life.*

Those are your two options, but you *never* say that you hate everyone and want everyone to fail. Most human beings are in that exact same position. No one is here for bad. Everyone is here for good.

Intentions can be twisted, causing confusion. If people are not feeding their bodies appropriately, taking care of their bodies and minds, even the best of intentions can destroy huge amounts of the world. Remember that everyone means well, and we all speak the same language underneath: we say and do what we think is best for ourselves. What we often hear are arguments about the advantages of gas-powered cars over electric, the need to preserve national parks, or the preference to let the national parks go. These specifics are part of the corporeal world, and our discussions can be confusing and divisive.

Understand that everyone intends good. If you keep that in mind, your angel can remember that we are all here for good and there is no reason to fear. Then, you can communicate better. If you can communicate clearly and cleanly, you've basically won the battle, because communicating your good intention can help people abandon their fear. They can act out of love instead of fear, in which case, amazingly divine things will occur.

Fear Hides Divinity

If you're scared, you're going to act from a place of self-preservation, for security instead of growth. Your divine self wants to grow and ascend. You want to achieve great things. When you entered this world, you were full of wonder. Maybe your dreams have been dashed, or something you tried didn't work out, and you lost confidence. You decided to stop trying, and all you wanted to do was protect yourself. It's as if you calloused your life. You had to cushion the blow, in case something else bad happened.

Understand that your divine purpose is everything that you've ever wanted. You can stop being afraid and understand that events not exactly to your liking are helping guide you to your optimal purpose, to your end game. You should let fear drip off. Let fear go away.

Again, you can achieve everything that you want. Every day, you can work at achieving. Maybe you don't know yet what your actual purpose is, but you are thinking about it. Keep trying and let the fear go away. Rip the armor off and go for it. It's amazing what you can achieve.

You may find out that your purpose wasn't what you thought it was. Give it all you have, and then you let your divine self guide you upward. Sure, you may not initially achieve what you thought you were going to, but your purpose will become clear at the end. You will achieve everything you need, and all your hopes and dreams will be met.

Recognition of Love Everywhere

You need to decide that every single person is intending good things. Love is everywhere, and it doesn't matter if someone's got a gruff demeanor or they say things that hurt your feelings. They don't *mean* that. It is not about you. They have their own problems, some hazy lens through which they see the corporeal world. They say things that they don't realize are going to be hurtful.

They may need a light turned on.

I'm more of a cerebral person than my wife. When we got married, I thought all the time and didn't have a lot of feelings. I wasn't able to share my heart and wonder how another person feels. I was always thinking about the next logical step without worrying. Being married to my wife has helped me understand that people do have feelings, and it's given me feelings as well. The birth of my children gave me this incredible warmth of love inside.

Understand that love is everywhere. No matter what someone says, you can laugh to yourself. If a guy pulls his car in front of you and gives you the finger, remember there's something going on in him that has nothing to do with you.

Every single time someone upsets you, you can let that go and tell yourself: *There's love there. It's not about me.*

They are confused in their life, in which case, they're coming at you. Maybe you miscommunicated. Maybe you have a problem, and this person thinks you're trying to be intentionally harmful. Clearly there is miscommunication. Maybe you need to explain that your point is not to hurt, but to do good. Explain what you're trying to do, and acknowledge that the other person sees it a different way. The issue becomes communication, not a personal conflict.

Recognize love everywhere. Recognize that no one intentionally wakes up in the morning and says they're going to hurt you. Live out your life. Let the fear go away. Live out your life, and you will achieve everything that you've ever wanted to achieve.

If you understand we're all here for good, if you recognize that there's love everywhere, and if you can get rid of fear, you can achieve everything—anything and everything you want. Mind you, it may not be what your mind believes that you want. It may be what God believes that you want. It may be what your angel is trying to let you know.

Maybe you'll travel through trials while you're trying to achieve your purpose, but if you keep your mind open to the fact that everything will work out, nothing bad will happen. Things will be as they will be. You will live a better existence. You can let anxiety fade. You can truly focus on achieving without worrying about failing.

The most successful people in the world have two things in common: they make quick decisions, and they have mentors. If you want to achieve something great, talk to somebody who's already achieved it. They're going to help you. If you don't make a decision, you will never go anywhere.

So just make the decision that you think is right. If you can make a decision—whether you fail or not—you're going in the correct direction; you will learn. If you don't make any decision at all, you'll never go anywhere, and you'll never achieve anything.

CHAPTER SIX

Nourishing Your Being (Diet)

EATING REAL FOOD

Clearly, our country and our world have a problem with food being engineered and chemically created. It's seldom that you walk into a store and the majority of the food that you see is *actual* food! Most foods are processed, packaged in bags and boxes, bearing little resemblance to how it looked when it was grown or born.

I read this quote from Dr. Mark Hyman at drhyman. com: *If you walk into a grocery store and there's a small section that says the 'health food' section, what do you call everything else?*

Clearly there's a problem because you should be eating to feed your being. You should be eating to fulfill a purpose. If what you're putting into your body is *not* feeding your purpose, then it is directly antagonistic to your purpose.

Real Food Still Has Energy

My biochemistry professor in my doctoral studies said, "The whole reason we are here, the purpose of humans, is to create ATP."

ATP is energy for human beings. It's how we produce energy — how we walk, talk, think, everything. Without ATP, we are not alive. Real food still has energy. It actually feeds your being. Now, you can eat calories, fat, protein, carbohydrates, and alcohol without consuming real food.

Real food contains other helpful chemicals that scientists call *free radicals*. They are naturally occurring chemicals that offset some of the oxidation, or radical energy. You've probably heard that free radicals damage your health, and you need antioxidants to protect you from the free radicals. The truth is, if we're eating real food, that food already contains antioxidants to offset the free radicals. Taking a bunch of antioxidants as a supplement after the oxidation has already occurred may not have any benefit at all.

Eating real food will *feed* your ability. It has energy in it to protect you and to reinforce your abilities to achieve whatever you want to achieve. Eat fruits, vegetables, nuts, seeds, and meat. Eat foods you could eat directly off a tree or right out of the ground, or as soon as it starts walking on the ground. Eating a lot of different,

Nourishing Your Being (Diet)

other foods — things like grains — requires preparation. They're sold in bags and boxes. With beans, you need to soak and cook them. You can even eat meat raw, if you take proper care. It will help further your ability to fulfill your purpose.

What to Eat

A young lady I went to college with said her mom always told her that if you only eat what grows from the ground, or what has a mother, you're going to be just fine.

That's true to an extent, but try limiting your food to:

- Fruits
- Vegetables
- Nuts
- Seeds
- Meat

You'll be in good shape. Other foods that don't fall exactly into these guidelines can still keep you healthy, but as a good rule, this list should be the majority of your diet.

Now, if you want percentages for each category — because obviously there's an optimal amount — around 50 percent of your diet should be vegetables. Those are going to be full of antioxidants and they're low-calorie, so you're getting less of the free radicals that break

113

down your body and more antioxidants to offset those free radicals.

Eat about 25 percent meat, so you get proteins and fats, which *are* necessary. Low-fat diets *will* make you fat. Low-fat food will not feed your brain, or help you create hormones. If you are not eating fats—specifically animal fat—you are going to miss out. The animal needs to be appropriately raised to get the proper nutrients. We know a 100 percent grass-fed pasture-raised animal has a completely different nutrition profile than a grain-fed, feed-lot-fed, tortured animal. Meat from stressed animals is going to be inflammatory, whereas 100 percent grass-fed animal meat is anti-inflammatory.

Eat about 10 percent nuts and seeds, and about 15 percent fruits. Your fruits, although incredibly healthy, can also be high in sugar, so if you eat fruit all day long, you will hurt the sugar profile in your body. You will increase the amount of insulin. Fruit contains a lot of fructose, so it's likely you'll end up depositing fat in your liver.

We all know the liver does a whole lot—most people say detoxification—but really it does everything:

- It helps create neurotransmitters.
- It deaminates proteins, the building blocks of life.
- It detoxifies you.

If your liver becomes fatty, bad stuff begins.

Nuts and seeds are healthy, too. They contain good proteins and healthy fats. Ideally, limit them to 10 percent, though, because they are also full of *phytic acid,* an anti-nutrient that stops the absorption of minerals like calcium, magnesium, iron, and zinc. Research shows that if you're eating a lot of phytate-containing foods—nuts, seeds, and foods I don't recommend like grains or beans—it will pull enough zinc out of your body to increase damage from illness. Also, if you're eating a lot of phytate-containing foods, you may suffer added liver damage due to hepatitis.

Feed the Child

In addition to fueling your body and fulfilling your purpose, one of the things that we talk about at our clinic is scheduling freedom. You don't want to constantly focus on improving yourself and never enjoy what you have. When I say *feeding your child,* I want you to enjoy what you're eating. So, put some time into it. Put some love into it.

You could buy a bunch of vegetables at the store and eat them all week, along with an unseasoned hamburger patty. You would have the same plate of hamburger patties and a bunch of organic vegetables for every meal. You will be very healthy doing that, however, you're going to be missing out on enjoying what you eat, because you're doing it just to fuel yourself.

That's fine, but most people want to experience pleasure from all aspects of life:

- Their worth
- Their work
- Their hobbies
- Their food
- Their workouts
- Their sleep

They want to dream beautiful dreams. Every aspect of life should entail some pleasure.

So, while you're nourishing your being and feeding yourself within the framework of a perfect diet, you need to feed the child as well. If you keep the child happy, it won't disagree with what you're eating. If you add flavor by putting spices and seasoning into the hamburger patty and vegetables, you're clearly going to enjoy it more. You're going to look forward to that meal. As soon as you stop being able to look forward to things, you have no reason to continue. Having something to look forward to and having dreams and goals—short-term and long-term goals—gives you a reason to move forward.

When you feed the child, you feed the essence inside of your body that wants to feel pleasure. You can eat the correct foods, but season them up by looking for recipes that match your guidelines. There are cookbooks out there that follow the eating protocols I've described.

My wife is a chef; she went to culinary school. She has created a cookbook for the patients in my practice. Our patients can email a recipe that they're used to preparing — maybe their mom used to make it — and if it doesn't fit our protocol, my wife will email them back a recipe with substitutions. Typically, it will taste every bit as good; however, it will not only feed the child, but also feed the whole being.

EATING WITH COMPASSION

You should care about the way your food is treated, and that even means your vegetables.

Are you going to be happy about poison being sprayed all over your vegetables?

You may think it keeps the bugs away, so it's okay.

If there are no holes on your vegetables or fruit because the bugs can't eat it, why the heck are you going to eat it?

Food is food, and a bug wants to eat it as much as you do. When I go to a farmers' market, I ask the farmers if they spray their crops. I want to know if they put poison on it. If they say they don't, the first thing I do is look at their produce. If there are no holes in it, I don't want it. I will go to the farmer at the market who has the most holes in their vegetables, and that's what I will buy because it's something that humans are supposed to eat.

Have compassion for animals as well. Have compassion for the creatures who provide meat. If the animals are treated appropriately while alive, their meat is much better for you. By showing compassion, you are nourished more.

Respecting Our Food

A lot of my patients come in and say they don't eat red meat as if it's a badge of honor. Research is being released stating that red meat will cause colon cancer and all sorts of problems. They say it's not healthy; you shouldn't eat red meat. Here's the deal: if you're eating typical feedlot-raised meat, you're more likely to get colon cancer and all sorts of other cancers.

The fat content in a feedlot, grain-fed cow is unhealthy. Cows are not meant to eat grain, they're meant to eat grass; it's what they eat naturally. We know that omega-3s are anti-inflammatory, and we know that omega-6s are inflammatory. In order to be optimally healthy and control inflammation, human beings need one omega-3 for every two-to-three omega-6s in their diets. A cow that has been grain-fed has around one omega-3 to twenty omega-6s, so you become much more inflamed after eating the meat. With 100 percent grass-fed cattle, the ratio is one to two, or one to three. It's perfectly suited for human beings to eat. There is nothing wrong with it. That is respecting your food.

Chickens are meant to run around in a field. They're not meant to be stuck in a feed lot with their beaks seared off, with their feathers plucked out, stuffed in a cage that's one foot wide, all smacked together. It's a stressful life, and every time caged chickens eat, they feel pain. The fat from these chickens is unhealthy. It's incredibly inflamed.

Do you want to know why so many chickens have salmonella?

Living in that stressful environment over their entire lives, they have no immune system. So, just as a human would get salmonella, chickens can get it, too. Most chickens in a feedlot environment were stuffed into cages and tortured their whole life. They have no immune system to fight salmonella, so when you eat it, you must cook it well, otherwise you're likely to get salmonella.

Eggs can also give you salmonella. A pasture-raised bird who runs around in the field, eats grubs, and is fed organic food produces meat full of omega-3s. Their immune systems are stronger. The chances of a pasture-raised chicken carrying salmonella are slim. It's important to respect your food. When animals are respected, their meat is much healthier to eat.

You Are What You Eat

Another factor to consider is hormonal release. Let's say your boss yells at you at work. Then, on the drive home, cars cut you off in traffic. You arrive home, and the dog is barking. Your spouse yells at you. You are stressed. You secrete something called cortisol, a stress hormone. Stress hormones are fat-based. Most of them are cholesterol-based.

The fats stored in cows and chickens that are tortured their whole lives and not allowed to live in a natural environment are full of a stress hormone. That hormone will be in their meat, so when you eat it, it will actually stress you. If you're eating that meat, you're more likely to deal with your life in a stressed-out manner. Your own stressors become amplified because you already have stress hormone from another animal inside your body, not to mention the added inflammation. Your food adds stress on your biochemistry and physiology.

You are what you eat. If you are eating chemical-laden fruits and vegetables that are full of pesticides and genetically modified crops, you are eating things that don't belong in the human body. Obviously they don't belong in the human body, so you, in turn, feel like you don't belong in the world. Life seems difficult. All you want to do is get home and go to bed at night. You don't really have a reason for being.

After a while, you'll get sick. The human body is not meant to process those unhealthy substances, and your body will try to get rid of them. It's an adaptation. You are what you eat, because you really *are* what you eat. It doesn't change. If you eat inflamed meat, you become inflamed. If you eat very healthy food, you become very healthy. It's black and white.

Modern human beings are the sickest species to ever walk the planet. It's not a genetic issue. If it were, our ancestors would have been as sick. I've heard people say that we live so much longer than our ancestors lived. That's not true either. When we account for decreased childhood mortality — which was significantly greater historically than it is now — and adjust for that, we actually live one *less* year of life than our ancestors did. People are saying the increased numbers in cases of cancer, autism, and all these other inflammatory diseases is because we can diagnose them better. That's *not* the truth. The truth is we've become out of touch with how human beings are supposed to live. Our bodies are creating more and more adaptations, and those adaptations are called disease.

Compassion for Food Brings Compassion for Self

If you have compassion for everything around you, you are having compassion for yourself, because you're connected to everything. The universal subconscious connects you with all things. Spirit moves through all things. When you're walking around every day, think compassionately about everything else. Have compassion for yourself.

The more you think about good things, the more optimistic you are. Studies have proven it.

Let's say in the morning you begin with gratitude statements such as:

- I'm so lucky to have my arms and legs, to be able to move however I want.

- I'm thankful to have a roof over my head.

- I'm so lucky to know where my next meal will come from.

- I'm living a heavenly existence.

The more you focus on gratitude, the less you stress about other things. You probably aren't going to be as judgmental of others either, because you're not worried about your own existence. Typically, when you judge yourself harshly, you judge other people harshly as well. Remember, if you judge other people, it means you're judging yourself. If you can have compassion for other people, and not judge them — understanding that everyone means well — then you end up not judging yourself. That's the beginning of a union of peace and harmony for the whole world.

EATING WITH PURPOSE

Eating with purpose includes knowing that everything you put in your mouth will do one of two things: it will either move you towards your goal of greatness, or it will push you in the direction of failure, not achieving what you want, and losing your purpose. Eating with a purpose is as important as living every day with a purpose. You recognize by now that your purpose is important. Eating is one thing you can do to help yourself achieve more. Keep that in mind — everything you put in your mouth affects you. You should realize that at all times.

Creating a Spark

Many different religions pray over their food before they eat. That prayer is trying to create a spark, adding to the energy needed to fulfill your purpose. Think about everything you put into your mouth. Ask yourself if this food is going to move you toward achievement.

What do you want to do?

Perhaps you want:

- To make the swim team
- To write a beautiful poem
- To be a great dancer
- To fly a plane

Everything you put into your mouth should create this spark, the energy for you to do what you want. Every time you eat try to feel lucky that you are able to put food into your mouth. Promise yourself to use the amazing gift of being fed and not starving to death to create greatness, to create a spark in the world, to lift people up, and to bring light into the darkness.

The food you put in your mouth should create a spark. You can eat an ice cream sundae with all the works but there's no energy or life for you in the cup. You're probably going to develop a stomachache, and then you're going to lie down and not move. You're probably not going to sleep well. You'll be a little more irritable.

You'll be more inflamed. That food is not going to lead you to save this world. It is not going to lead you to bring light into the darkness. It's not going to do what you need. But if you eat pure, organic, real food, you can help achieve all the great things that you're here for — your entire purpose.

Proliferating Perceptive Perfection

As you eat beautiful foods and feel energized by them, you realize that everything you put into your body can help proliferate your purpose. Another way to proliferate your purpose is by cleaning the lens that allows your soul to see into this world. If you can see into this world and see the truth, you need never doubt your purpose again. You never doubt what you want, your dreams, or your goals.

You should never have to check in with someone to ask if your plan sounds good or is a righteous path. You don't need to visit every guru, swami, or yogi to find your correct path, because you've become your own yogi, your own shaman, your own leader. You've cleaned your lens by creating perceptive perfection. You can perceive the world in such a crystal-clear, immediate moment. You can see it for what it is.

All your senses are keen. Your nerves work right. Your cardiovascular system works right. Your brain works right.

You will never doubt yourself again if you always work to create perceptive perfection:

- By eating appropriately
- By creating the spark
- By having compassion for your world
- By knowing and living your purpose
- By being gracious

You'll be a happy person. You won't need to tell people what you do or who you are. You will be yourself, and people will notice it and tell you. You won't have the insecurity that leads to explaining what you like to do. You *become* that, so you won't need to go around trying to advertise yourself. You become a remarkable person, and people remark about you, regardless.

Unlimited

Once you've created perceptive perfection everything is keen, everything is bright. You've brought light, and everything is unlimited. There is no reason to fear anymore. You don't have to fear anything. You will be clear and see only love in the world. You've become unlimited in your potential to do anything you want. You are made to achieve everything you want. Perceptive perfection allows you to see the truth of what you want.

Suppose a person with a terrible voice thinks they want to be a great and famous singer. Chances are that's not their purpose here on Earth. They were *not* brought here for a purpose they can never achieve. When you are in perceptive perfection, your main interest will be your purpose. You become unlimited in your ability to achieve it. The ability of your body will match your purpose.

You won't feel alone anymore, because you'll fit within:

- The puzzle of the universe
- The puzzle of the relationship that you want
- The puzzle of the life you want
- The puzzle of where to live

It all becomes clear. It all works out. If you look at a picture, and your vision is blurred, nothing is crisp. You might think you're seeing the wrong picture because it doesn't make sense. But if your vision is clear, it's a beautiful picture. The pieces will fit together perfectly, down to the last detail. Your life can be the same. All you need to do is feed your body, exercise your body, think in a way that does create perceptive perfection, and all of your dreams can come true.

Do not eat to be social. Eating to be social is a part of our modern human world. Our ancestors used to eat because they had a big kill and they were starving, and they all ate to celebrate. Now, your celebrations don't need to include food, although that is a natural human tendency. When you eat, it shouldn't be because someone brought you a cheeseburger; don't eat it to be gracious.

Instead, be excited to eat with your friends, and to help them in a way that will help feed their purpose and their perceptive perfection. When you have control over food choices, you should not give people food that's going to destroy their purpose. Instead, feed them — your kids, your friends, your family, your parents, all of them — feed them food that will fulfill their purpose and create that spark.

CHAPTER SEVEN

Exercising Your Being

PUSHING YOUR LIMITS

Pushing your limits is important because if you are not achieving or moving forward, you're falling behind. Existence continues to grow and evolve. You need to grow, evolve, and change at the same level as, or greater than, the rest of existence. Suppose you sit down on your couch and decide that you are happy with everything you've accomplished, and instead of continuing to work out and eat right you are going to watch TV and eat whatever you want. You stop exercising. Suppose you tell yourself that you are content with how far you've come.

You cannot stay still. Your body and world are constantly changing, and you would end up losing the health you worked for. You would become unhappy and not confident. You would end up breaking yourself back down. If you are not constantly pushing your limits, and forcing yourself to grow, you are dying. Push your limits.

Achievement Brings Achievement

Your body, like a child, will give you back talk. It will tell it doesn't want to do this or that. The more you can push your body and yourself to achieve in this world, the more it becomes a habit. The less you push yourself to achieve great things, the more that child talks back. The child's voice, your body's voice, becomes stronger; continually saying it doesn't want to exercise. It doesn't want to eat right. It becomes stronger and stronger, repeating that it doesn't want to do what you need. It wears you down. Your guardian angel finally decides to stop fighting and tells that child to go ahead.

Every day you're building habits. If you let the voice tell you no and you say okay, that's a habit. But, the more you refuse to give into that voice because you realize the need to achieve and work for your goals and purpose, the more you gain. Then, you're building a way of being. The more the voice wins, the greater the habit of losing. The habit of *not* growing becomes your norm. When you push through that, growing becomes your norm.

If you consistently tell a child what needs to happen over and over again, eventually they will stop arguing. You can get your body to do the same thing. You can get that negative part of your being to go away because it already knows what you are going to do. Your body will learn that you are going to get up and work out. It will expect you to eat the right foods. It will not expect trash at McDonald's or Burger King.

Today, promise yourself to speak with integrity at all times. Say what you mean, and mean what you say. Don't give in to that voice that wants to go the other way. Don't give in to the voice that wants to do the wrong thing. Achievement will bring achievement because the easier it gets, the more you'll want to achieve. It becomes who you are. It's a habit of winning.

A Reservoir of Happiness

When I achieve a goal, I typically feel good about it. When I reflect on my day it feels good to know:

- I didn't eat that donut.
- I ate all the things I should eat.
- I spoke kindly to my wife and told her how great she is.
- I told my kids how great they are.
- I pushed through my highly stressed self and played with my kids.

When I sit down on my bed at night after I've done all that and achieved all those goals, I am happy. I'm content with my life. I know that I have what it takes to succeed.

After doing this for a long time, that childlike voice goes away. Succeeding every day, all the time, creates a reservoir of happiness. You create happiness knowing that you have already won the battle.

My son came in the bedroom at 3:30 in the morning after I had gone to bed at ten o'clock the other night. I knew I wanted to work out at 5:00 a.m. He didn't let me sleep the rest of the night. He had his feet on me, kicking me, talking to me, rubbing my face. Now my son's a toddler, and he irritated me the whole night. I took great happiness and pleasure from the fact that I got up at 4:45 to work out. I was tired, but I knew that it was not an option to say no to working out. That's it.

I created a pure feeling of achievement because I still worked out even though I was so tired. I was so proud of myself that it created a positive energy, a kind of sunshine inside of me. For the rest of my day, there was no way I was going to lose. I overcame the hardest point of the day. I won.

Understand that you can do the same thing as I did. You can focus your mind on achievement, and take pleasure from that focus, knowing it creates a whole reservoir for happiness. Achievement breeds achievement. Happiness will breed happiness. Basically, you can live a heavenly existence here on Earth.

Expansion of the Reservoir

You can create this reservoir of happiness, and it can exceed any limits you had in your mind. It's okay to feel happy all the time. You don't have to punish yourself every time something doesn't go your way. Typically, when something doesn't go your way, it steers you in a direction that is a better path anyway. Keep this in mind, and keep yourself happier and happier each day, achieving more and more.

You now want to see your friends and family achieve more. You want to see people that you've never met achieve more. You're not going to judge people for their way of life.

Why would you?

You're already happy with your life. The most judgmental people in the world are not happy with their lives. It's just the way it is. Because they're unhappy, they want to find reasons to speak badly about other people because that makes them feel better. They try to stop other people from running up the mountain so it looks like they're higher than others.

To expand your reservoir of happiness, you can help coach and mentor other people. You can push other people to achieve. If they want to run up the mountain, help drag them along with you as you climb. It doesn't matter what's going on with other people. You're happy for yourself, so you're happy to see other people succeeding as well. The expansion of the reservoir of happiness continues because even on those days where something happens that you weren't expecting, the puzzle pieces are still fitting together.

We're creating a heavenly existence as a culture, as a people, as a world, as an existence. We expand that reservoir of happiness through *all* of eternity, and we basically build our road map to heaven.

EFFICIENT ENERGY FLOW

When pushing your limits trying to create all this happiness, understand that the more you push them, the greater the result. The more you exercise, the better you get at exercising. If you exercise on intense intervals, giving it all you have with intensity, your body and your cells will create more ATP per calorie.

The old model is one gram of carbohydrate equals four calories, one gram of fat creates nine calories, one gram of alcohol creates seven calories, and one gram of protein creates four calories. I had a biochemistry professor telling me at one point that the purpose of life is to create ATP, because ATP is energy. Push your limits every day; grow, work out, take care of yourself, and become more efficient in producing that energy.

At the end of your workday, you won't just fall asleep. You'll continue to live your life.

So many people go home and plop on the couch because they can't even move. They are too tired to be the parents or spouse they want to be. However, you absolutely can be efficient with your energy production. By pushing your limits, exercising your being, and pushing yourself to the limit, you can create energy more efficiently.

Ever Present and Undressed

Many of us wear a mask as we walk around in our daily life. We're pretending to be something we are not. Inside of you, in the deep dark corners of your mind, are *you* as you were meant to be. Maybe that version of you is so repressed that you don't even know who you are anymore, but you're there. You are, as you are right now, perfect. Be honest with yourself, take care of yourself, and do not spend energy on holding that in. Then you can shine. There's no reason to put the mask on. There's no reason to cover yourself up because you already fit within the puzzle.

When you were a kid, maybe you put on a show when you wanted attention from other kids, acting like something you didn't want to be. Maybe you were the bad kid who didn't get enough attention at home, so you wanted attention at school. Maybe you sought negative attention, but it wasn't really who you were. It wasn't who you wanted to be. You became that person because you wanted attention. And maybe that pattern continued for years on end.

You can drop it. Yeah, you're going to have to deal with a little bit of fallout, because your current friends probably aren't the friends you need to be with. You're drinking, you're smoking, and you're doing drugs because you can't have fun with these friends if you are yourself. The substances are a social lubricant. You don't need the social lubricant if you are yourself. When you hang out with people that are of like minds, they become your tribe.

I'm asking you to stop covering up who you are. I'm asking you to push yourself to the limits in the weight room. I'm asking you to push yourself to the limit in delayed gratification. Do what's right for your body so you can go out and become who you want to be. If you're always going to be there, you shouldn't be hiding.

Naked and Fearless

Once you undress your soul and show people who you are, you have a completely clear lens, and everyone can see you. You are naked, and you have no reason to fear anything.

Why would you fear anything if you are truly living your purpose?

If you are absolutely doing your best every day, there's no reason to fear anything. Let's say something happens that you did not want.

Are you going to get mad at God?

Are you going to get mad at the Universe and stamp your feet like a little child?

Or are you going to realize that the world does not revolve around you?

You are a part of the puzzle, here to fulfill your purpose. There is no reason to fear if you are being yourself, if you are doing your best. You should relish whatever comes, because you know it's going to drive you further towards your utopia, your happiness, your heaven.

When I say *naked and fearless*, I mean your soul is exposed. Everyone can see you for who you are. I'm asking you to be who you are. Optimize who you are. Push your limits, grow to the best thing you can be, and try to help everyone else be the best they can be. You never have to fear again in your life.

You can always communicate, always be happy, always be confident, and help all your loved ones do the same. You will need to strip down. You will go through some obstacles that you have created yourself by not being you. In the end, you will find happiness—truly find your happiness.

EXERCISING FOR PURPOSE

Many of us don't want to exercise. You had a bad night of sleep; you want to sleep in. You don't want to work out. You were with the kids during the day, you're tired at night and don't want to work out then. But if you keep in mind that you're not just exercising for a purpose in the future, but actually going to have a better day immediately, it makes it easier to get to the gym. You will find that when you go to the gym to work out, or go outside running, or wherever you do it — even if you stay at home doing pushups on the floor—that you are pushing yourself towards something good.

Nothing bad is coming from exercising, unless we do it, say, for ego purposes. If you want to be the strongest person on the planet so you can say you lifted the heaviest weight, you might injure yourself. But, if you're exercising smart, you're taking care of yourself. The purpose of exercising is to make you the person you want to be, to help you unveil the greatest you that you can be, so you can fulfill your purpose.

Recognition of Purpose

The first thing you need to do is recognize your purpose. I'm a doctor, and I want to help people get well. I want to empower people to change their lives. I don't want them to be sick and on drugs their whole life, their power taken away because another doctor told them they would be on medication for their whole life and never feel well.

I had a hand that was swollen with inflammation from psoriatic arthritis. I couldn't open it up until the end of the night. I couldn't turn the doorknob; I couldn't open the pickle jar. I had psoriasis from head to toe, diarrhea all the time, and acid reflux. I was on many medications.

If I keep exercising hard, eating well, and maintaining my mental awareness, that stuff goes away. I must exercise every day for my purpose. I recognize that my purpose is to inspire and change people's lives so that we can make this whole world a healthier place where fulfilling one's purpose is much easier. That recognition of purpose propels me to go to the gym in the morning, even when I'm tired.

In addition to my purpose of making the world a healthier place, it is my purpose to be a great husband, a great father, and friend. When I recognize that I am not just working out for me, but for my loved ones as well, it becomes a *must*. I must exercise. I must get up in the morning.

If I exercise first thing in the morning, I give myself an extra cortisol rush. Cortisol helps keep you alert throughout the day, and it's inversely related to something called melatonin, which puts you to sleep at night. It's called a circadian rhythm: high cortisol in the morning, high melatonin at night. I go to sleep like a baby, and I jump out of bed like a lion to go serve my purpose in the morning.

Exercise in the morning will help you fortify your routine. You need to recognize your purpose in order to exercise consistently.

Pushing the Boundaries

When you exercise, you must constantly push your limits to keep growing. Let's say you are bench-pressing one hundred pounds, and you do three sets of ten, every single day. After a while, the gain will stop, and your body will come back down. You cannot lift the same amount of weight all the time, or decrease.

The whole universe is growing, and you have to grow with it. You can't stop growing; you must keep pushing. I don't mean growing in size or equipment. If you want to do yoga all the time, you're not going to become a big, muscular person. The idea is to push yourself further than you were the last time—to be stronger, to be more balanced. Give it that much more, because you're not just pushing the boundaries of your physical exercise, but your mental state as well.

Let's say the furthest you've ever run is a mile. If you run that mile, and that's all you've ever run, you can push your boundary by telling yourself to run one mile and one step. You just achieved something new. Star Trek would call it *the final frontier*. This isn't the final frontier but a next step into new territory. You just made a step you haven't made before. That's exciting. It creates happiness, and helps you proliferate more exercise and more expression of your overall being.

Creating New Purpose

As you push your limits and achieve new things, your body will be capable of doing physical and spiritual things you never thought were possible. As you keep pushing your limits, your achievements and success will keep growing until it becomes a habit.

Let's say you couldn't stand up for more than a minute because you were so ill. When you are able to stand again, it feels great. Instead of walking down the block for energy or exercise, you decide to try a yoga class. Now you are standing for an hour, so you are confident that you can perform different postures. You create a new purpose not only to go for a walk, but also to stand on one leg, close your eyes, and not fall over.

A person who suffers from neuropathy overcomes the burning, aching, and numbness. They've achieved one purpose. They can stand and walk without pain or problems; they can actually live. Now they can push it; to see how far they can get away from sickness.

To be super healthy or super-duper fit means you're not sick. As your body grows healthier and can walk further, you might decide to jog instead of walk down the block.

Maybe you're eighty years old, and you're doing something you haven't done for thirty years. Well, congratulations! You had your purpose: being able to stand and walk around the field to watch your grandson play baseball. Now you can pick up a baseball and throw the baseball back and forth to your grandchild. You're capable of this. Playing catch becomes a new purpose, a new boundary to beat. Once you beat that, you can beat the next one. That, too, becomes a habit. It's an amazing thing, to realize that everything is purpose-driven. As soon as you can achieve one goal, you can achieve the next.

CHAPTER EIGHT

Connecting With Your Being

YOUR BEING IS YOUR EGO

I think it's important to understand why we're here. We could all be part of everything without being conscious of our own being or ego. Yet, we *are* here feeling pains and struggles, but also feeling triumphs; pride, and love. Our being is our way of trying to show everyone how great our spirit is. We are here for purpose.

Your ego is your body; you're here to show and reflect to everyone who and how great you are. If you're not taking pride in yourself, no one will see that reflection of greatness.

We Are Infinite

We are all part of that which is infinite. We are all part of a universal subconscious, a divine being. I strongly believe—and I think you will, too—that we manifest ourselves into this reality, this corporeal world, this playground to reflect greatness. We show people who we are to help them reflect their own greatness and bring them into a greater existence. At the end of our corporeal life, this consciousness, we *die*, but that does not mean we are gone. We move back into the universal subconscious, the infinite—God, love, and all great things—without our ego, and that's okay.

It's like diving into a swimming pool and becoming the water. You flow with everything else. You are part of it; you still exist. We are infinite in the same way. At any point in time, you can jump back out of the water. You can take your water molecules, bring them back out onto the surface, and become part of the world after enjoying your heaven—being part of the infinite, God, and love. You could jump back out of the water to experience your ego and your being once again. This process never ends, because we are infinite. Basically, you decide when you choose to experience your ego once again in the corporeal world. Heaven, however, is eternal.

Our Ego Is Conscious

What you see in the mirror is your body, which is helping manifest your spirit into this world. Your body has its own consciousness and is conscious of the world. It binds with you, and you're aware of it.

The ego walks around and creates judgments and worries, things that are not productive for greatness. Your ego wonders if you're pretty or handsome enough. Your ego worries that you're fat, skinny or pale. When you walk down the street and meet someone coming toward you, your ego might question if that person is going to hurt you. You experience fear. That is not your infinite being talking. That is the ego, which is your body, manifesting within. Those words that you're thinking are not really you; they are your ego speaking to you.

Your ego is like a child; it needs to be taught. It needs to be educated on what's proper and what's not. It is improper to allow fear to guide your life, to let negativity choose your path. As you reflect your greatness, you should bring light into focus. You should bring greatness into this world, and that includes bringing greatness to your ego.

If your ego is being guided by fear, insecurities, and negative thoughts, then you're not bringing light to your ego. Your ego is then left to wander in darkness. It's up to you to bring light to that darkness, and shut off those negative thoughts and insecurities.

When your child does something wrong, you don't judge your child. You want the best for them; you think your child is the best thing in the world. You want to guide them to a positive place without judging them.

The same thing works with your thoughts. As negative thoughts roll through your mind asking you to doubt your worth, keep in mind the voice is not you. These are fears from the past or anxiety about the future speaking, and you need to not judge them, but rather help rework them. Look at them and realize that this is not a positive route, and steer them in a different direction.

Entertainment for Eternity

We can feel blissful. We can feel heaven. We can feel infinitely tiny sensations all over our skin as an orgasmic experience—beautiful, overwhelming, and an ebullition of energy coming out of us. As human beings, our thoughts creep in and pull us into our ego. The more we accept ourselves as individuals rather than part of the whole, the more we come out into the world. It's the way we experience life and our own individualities from the whole.

Though we are all one, we have our own conscious point. That's what life really is; it's an entertainment for eternity. You see what you can achieve, see what you can do, see whom you can help to achieve, and bring more happiness and love into this environment as an individual. It's a beautiful thing. This entertainment for eternity never goes away.

Now, when you go back into the pool of the universal subconscious—God, love, and all great things—the one thing you must surrender is the ego. You can be eternally blissful, but you're not conscious of it. You feel it, but you're no longer an individual who consciously thinks about it. That becomes that entertainment of leaving the pool, analyzing the feelings we experience and putting meaning to them. The ego naturally does that. The key is to not allow the ego to start projecting a negative forecast ahead of you because of past trials and situations. If you do, you miss living in the present, in which great things are happening.

I put my hand on the counter in front of me, and it feels cold and smooth. That's a sensation. Now I can choose to label the sensation as nice or no big deal. We can find a way to love every single thing in our ego, love everything within this corporeal world—every little thing. I look at the wall, and it's got a smudge on it. That smudge can be an annoyance, or I can decide that smudge is beautiful, a divine creation for my pleasure and entertainment.

You can make this world—even as an ego, part of the corporeal world—a beautiful thing every day. If you decide to love every single thing around you at all times, never judging, you've created a corporeal world, which is also heavenly. Therefore, living as an ego can be just as beautiful as the universal subconscious, God, or the Divine. We can experience this beauty as an ego and also enjoy thinking about how beautiful the experience is instead of being part of it.

FULFILLING YOUR PURPOSE FEEDS YOUR EGO

Understand that your ego has purpose in this corporeal world:

- To help itself grow
- To help everything grow around it
- To help other people see the light within everything
- To stamp out the darkness within the corporeal world

While you're here you must achieve, you must do great things, and you must seek out everything that will bring greatness to the being you embody. You must keep the cycle going to make this world better and better. After you've experienced your next heaven, you want to come back into a more beautiful world; you want a world where it's easier to find light and happiness within every day.

The Being Has Purpose

I was born to two parents who struggled. They struggled to ensure our family functioned and struggled to make a living. We grew up poor, and it was hard on them. My dad hated the fact that he had to work all the time to make ends meet. He never got to spend time with his own kids, and my mom had to take care of all three of us—my brother, my sister, and me. My dad wanted to ensure we had a mother at home to take care of us. She had to work to help make ends meet as well. It was difficult for them.

One purpose I had in this world was to bring light to my parents who were steeped in the darkness of the corporeal world because their struggles were so great. They needed to see me becoming successful, helping people. I got to help my parents with their issues. There's nothing more fulfilling than being able to look back and realize that my parents were first there to mentor me beyond the difficulties they had, and now I get to help them out of the mud so that they can feel great again.

These purposes I share are very concrete. I knew I needed to make a great living and help a lot of people, because that brought light to my parents. Now, my parents can help reflect that light to other people, and bring more light into the world. I have children who are part of me, part of my life. I know I need to help them bring more light than I'm able to do.

I work for a world where no one is blocking anyone else's light, a world where people can disagree and still help others achieve their goals. I want to tell people they can swing their fists in the air as hard as they want, as long as they never touch my nose. I'm not here to stop anyone from living their life or inhibit them from finding their light. That's a corporeal understanding of the world we live in.

The Angel Has Purpose

I use the term angel to describe the actual spirit that embodies your ego. You, the angel, have a purpose here. Your ego has purpose here. The body that we fill has a purpose, and so does the angel who is here to help guide your body in this heavenly path. As an angel, one of your purposes is to help derail any negative thoughts that are possessive.

I was born into a chaotic situation where we struggled to get good food. We didn't get to go out often, we didn't take plane rides, and we didn't get nice things. That's not a big deal, but my ego held onto that chaos. I struggled. Perhaps I didn't want to share with other kids because I worried my toy would be broken. I wouldn't get a new toy. I didn't want to let kids into my parents' house, because I was afraid they might break something, and my parents wouldn't be able to replace it. We didn't have the money to do that. These are thoughts from my being, but as the angel, I must rise above them.

You must not judge past experiences and carry them into the future.

Leave behind:

- Negativity
- Insecurities
- Anger
- Fear

These emotions hold down the light that's trying to escape from you. As an angel, your work is to ensure your ego fulfills its purpose. You should also be able to enjoy everything that your ego is helping you experience in this corporeal world.

You Are One and the Same

Your body is the temple that houses God, the universal subconscious. You and the universal subconscious are one and the same. Your ego moves through the world finding its purpose. It will experience pleasure and wonderful things; it will also experience fear, pain, and disappointment. It's important for the angel to stand behind your creature and not allow those experiences to stop you.

If experience *did* stop you from achieving greater things, as an angel, you would not be able to experience all the great things that your ego offers. The purpose of the angel and being are one and the same. This is our entertainment for eternity.

You are on this planet to experience greatness as an ego, individually, as one single consciousness. You experience everything the world offers and make it heavenly. But you also need to ensure that, as the angel, your being achieves its purpose, walking you through fields of flowers. Your ego should surround you with people who love you and give love and reflect their light back to you. Your ego and angel are the same. They work together, so no matter what your child decides to do, the angel must act like a parent. Then, your child brings the parent along to experience all the great things that this world offers.

FULFILLING YOUR PURPOSE FEEDS THE UNIVERSAL SUBCONSCIOUS

We are all connected by God, by the universal subconscious in the spiritual world As you fulfill your purpose as child and angel, the light you create travels back through your roots, back into the universal subconscious. Light doesn't just shine out into the corporeal world; light shines back into the universal subconscious, helping feed the rest of the roots that grow trees out into the corporeal world. Fulfilling your purpose feeds the universal subconscious.

Helping Me Helps Us All

If I'm walking down the street and fall over, someone will probably grab me and ask if I'm okay. They show a warm or caring side of this world. This organic experience of lifting each other up is cyclical. As I am helped, I'll turn to someone else to help them, and it keeps going. Warmth feeds through me and becomes part of everything else. Warmth travels the loop into the spiritual world and then back out into the corporeal world. Every time I'm helped it feels like being dipped into that pool of divine energy, and it adds light. I'm bleeding more light on the page.

It's like a paintbrush on a paint wheel. I touch the paint with the paintbrush, and then back on the paper, then back onto the paintbrush, then back on the paper. The more times I repeat this action, the more the page fills with color and life. If you help me, you help us all

Helping You Helps Us All

There is definitely darkness on Earth in the corporeal world. Multiplying the light that exists within us will help us all. My goal each day is to help five different people and cause exponential growth amongst our whole species or consciousness. It's hard to stop the positivity from happening.

Just as I was helped after falling on the side of the street, I would do the same for you. If I help you, and you thank me and show gratitude, I will feel good about what I've done. Helping you has helped me. It's back and forth, back and forth. We create rings, a perfect circle of energy.

Helping me helps us all. Helping you helps us all. We are truly one in the same. We have different consciousness, but God, the divine entity connects us in the universal subconscious. We are always all connected.

I'll Meet You on the Other Side

Imagine for a moment a bright, sunny day with grass on the ground and a lake in front of you. There's a beautiful breeze, and it feels great. Let's say it's seventy-six degrees. Then, the flat ground begins to turn on an axis, like a metal lever flipping around. As it flips around, you begin in one place, and you dive back down through the grass and onto the other side when it flips over. Now you're in more of an energetic plane, where the spiritual energy exists.

Everyone can do that; it's like making love with the energy of the universe as you walk back through on the

Other Side. We decay as we leave our corporeal bodies, and we end up back in the universal subconscious. We will meet on the Other Side. We will be one on the Other Side. There is no more intimate place to exist than on the Other Side, where the ego's thoughts are no longer with us, but we feel all the incredibleness that is all things and everything, the infinite.

I'll meet you on the Other Side, and hopefully the Other Side is even more beautiful than it was the last time we were there. It is infinite, hard to understand because it exists within the energy of all things. We will feed the consciousness of the divine source, God, as we bring ourselves back into the universal subconscious. It is possible that change can occur within the infinite. Hopefully that change brings more warmth, more light, and more feelings of ecstasy through every single morsel of our being, even if we're not conscious of it on the Other Side.

CHAPTER NINE

Experiencing Your Heavenly Existence

ENJOYING THE PROCESS

You can work all day long, but in the end, if you only work, you can't enjoy the experience. We've often got our head down, our blinders on, and we're working hard. Perhaps you've dropped your belief in your own ability to be happy, and you're just keeping your head down while saying you don't want to be here anymore. You're just waiting until you die.

But this life is a blessing. I woke up this morning, I opened my eyes, and I thanked God that I got my first breath of the day. It's an incredible feeling to be here, and know that nothing bad is going to happen to you. The only bad thing that could happen is if you lose confidence in yourself and stop trying to achieve your purpose.

At some point in your life, you'll reach for something, and you're going to fail. Remember that the most successful people in the world fail multiple times before they succeed. When they succeed, they're great at it. You fail in order to succeed, and you should never be scared of failure.

You should look at the failure as a gift; you learned how to succeed by finding where your faults were, where things weren't going to work. The only time that you lose and truly fail is when you think you're not good enough or smart enough because events don't go your way. If you believe you can't do it, you quit. As long as you have a breath in your lungs, you can keep going. You can keep achieving. There's no reason, ever, to believe you've failed. Everything is attainable.

Being Conscious of This Reality Is Already a Blessing

When you were given the opportunity to step into the corporeal world or your ego, you were given an opportunity to be aware of your own existence. It is a blessing to be here and aware of that existence. You make choices for your individual spiritual reality in this world, to attain whatever you want. It is heavenly.

To experience this world as a playground, you must first:

- Calm your fears
- Calm your anxieties
- Calm your depression

Then, you can understand that while you live in the concrete world, you truly exist in a spiritual reality within that world, and nothing bad will ever happen. If you can understand that all things are at your fingertips, this existence becomes a playground. It is a beautiful, unbelievable experience. You can ride the ride and swim through the sky any time you want. It's all available to you.

Every morning when you wake up, you should take a deep breath and thank God you're on the playground, able to do anything you want. You should take care of your temple, your body, and your mind. You need to be good to people. But outside of those tasks, you can literally do whatever you want:

- You can run like a child.
- You can play on the playground.
- You can go swimming.
- You can work out.
- You can talk to people.
- You can give and receive love.
- You can kiss your spouse and kids.
- You can enjoy your family and friends.

And you, the reader, have the amazing gift of reading this book, utilizing what you're learning, and using your faculties to achieve your purpose. Every day, you can look out and enjoy this world. It's not just about working for your goals; it's also about happiness and fun while you're working. Enjoy the journey; it's there in front of you.

Happiness Is a Choice

When things don't go right, it's easy to be unhappy. Maybe you didn't get the job you were applying for. Maybe you snag your coat as you leave the house, a snag that rips your coat. You get mad, you jump up and down, and you stomp our feet like a baby because you think the world should revolve around you, that you are the center of the universe. If it's not going right for you, it's the worst thing in the world. You hate your life. You have forgotten that this reality you live in is a gift and a blessing.

Knowing that you're connected to all other things in the world makes this response seem ego-centric, egotistical, and small-minded. So, something happened to your ego that you're not excited about. That's okay. Let's say you run out the door, and you're in a rush to work, your coat snags on the door, and it rips. You are upset because you have to go back inside. Maybe that snag was a divine intervention, stopping you from getting into your car, pulling out of the driveway, and getting into a head-on collision and dying. The truth is that everything is working for your benefit, and you need to stop trying to control the way the reality comes out. You can only do what you can do. The random is random. Nothing bad is going to happen.

You need to be able to step back and realize that things can happen regardless of your personal actions. Or, if you were rushing, maybe it was a sign for you to slow down. So many times we get into a bad mood or upset because we're going so fast we can't slow down and see that everything is really okay.

The key here would be to just slow down. Be okay with whatever happens during your day. Give your best always so you never have to wonder whether it was your fault or divine intervention. If something bad happens, okay. If you've done your best you don't have to question whether you could have done better. Everything will work itself out to the most blissful state possible for you in life.

Your perception can change in the blink of an eye. At this moment, there may be a starving child in this world that would give their life to live as you for one day. You're upset about that sandwich that you didn't want, because you wanted filet mignon. You had to eat a sandwich, and you're upset about it. Keep in mind that sandwich could keep some kid alive, or maybe feed an entire family. That food would be heavenly to them.

So yes, at any point in time, you can make the decision to be happy. If you tear your coat and you're upset — it's your new Gucci coat, or some fancy name brand — okay. You spent some money on it; it's a fancy coat. Great.

Do you know how many people in this world would give up their life to have that coat for a week, even ripped, because it would keep them warm and alive?

Let's not be so shallow to think that these little monetary losses we're having are the end of all things.

Happiness is a choice. You can choose to be happy at any point in time. Think about it every single morning when you wake up. Choose to be happy the entire day. Let's make it a challenge:

Can you be happy for a whole day?

Can you defeat those internal thoughts that come through your mind?

If you are upset about something, defeat it. You can be happy. You can choose to live in a way where everything that passes through your mind goes up towards heaven, instead of going downward.

One Breath Here Is a Gift

Take a deep breath for me. Breathe in really, really deep and let your lungs expand. You can actually feel the air that embraces the inside your bronchial tubes down to your alveoli, and crosses the membranes going into your bloodstream, to absorb the oxygen into your blood vessels. Then breathe back out, push all that air out, and you can feel it passing through your lungs on the way out, pushing the carbon dioxide out. It's a beautiful thing. Every breath is a gift.

Breathing is unique in that it's controlled either consciously or unconsciously. You can choose to breathe, breathing in and then breathing out, or you can breathe without thinking about it. Breath is fundamental to life. If you woke up one morning and you had one breath and then died, that one breath would still be a gift. You were able to visualize and see the wall, realize what color it is. You saw the topography of the wall. You discerned rough and smooth. All these things are entertainment for us.

You are so lucky that you were born into this life, and into a body. Let's say you have no arms and no legs.

You can go online and look at a YouTube video of a guy who says, "No arms, no legs, no problems."

He was born with no arms and no legs, but he's happy all the time.

Something beautiful that he said, which really touched me, was, "What kind of a husband am I going to be?

I can't even hold my wife's hand! What kind of a husband will I be to do that? But in the end, it won't matter, because in the end I will hold her heart."

There's so much more than the physical reality that's binding us. There's something we can all feel inside. It's such a beautiful thing, to have that one breath here.

This world can be an amazing place. The only thing that makes you see otherwise is fear. It's time to teach other people not to fear and raise other people up. As you raise them up, hopefully they will raise other people up, and we will keep spiraling up our existence. It's time to realize that one breath is a heavenly breath, every single morning when you wake up. Hopefully you can embrace that beauty and feel that every day as you live.

Remember that you should be looking at yourself and trying to push yourself forward to greater heights. You will make yourself a little uncomfortable at times so that you can force yourself to grow. But most of the time you're in this journey should be enjoyable. You should always view life as an enjoyable experience; something to learn from, something to achieve, something to experience as wonderful.

Please, please, wake up every morning, thank God for your ability to open your eyes, for your ability to take your first breath, and for your ability to go step out into the world. Enjoy the playground, and enjoy climbing the ladder towards your next heaven.

THERE IS NO WRONG PATH

When I was in a very dark place in my life, I was scared of so many things. I was worried that my future would be destroyed, and I'd never be able achieve anything. I feared I would never be able to become what I wanted to be, find a wife, or have children or a family. I worried that I didn't dress right, didn't look right, or say the right things.

I created a mantra to help me with that, and I would repeat it: *Nothing bad ever happens; everything always works out; and things will be as they will be.*

These words removed the pressure from worrying about what was going to happen next.

The truth is nothing bad is going to happen. Everything is going to work out. Things will be as they will be as long as you want them to, as long as you take one step. All you've got to do is take one step in the direction you want to go, and everything is going to be okay.

You need to make that push. Push yourself to believe that you have the ability to be happy in life. Trust yourself, knowing that you know best how to get yourself to that place. Taking a few steps in the right direction makes it that much easier to see that everything is going to be okay.

Nothing Bad Ever Happens

I say nothing bad ever happens, and it sounds callous.

You might ask:

- What about that person's baby dying?
- What about this war?
- What about other terrible things?

I feel bad that these realities exist. I also know that they create fear in us, and that we need to overcome the fear. One of the things about living in the corporeal world is we must overcome a lot. The whole world is full of possibilities, but we need to overcome so many things in order to achieve them. The first thing to overcome is the fear.

You feel bad that someone lost a limb or someone's sick. It's hard to watch someone that you love hurting. It's hard to watch anybody go through times that are hard, painful, or sad. These emotions exist because their opposites exist: bliss, glee, and health.

Remember the guy in "No Arms, No Legs, No Problem." He has no arms and no legs. Maybe he used to feel bad for himself. Now, he is an incredible speaker who shows other people how to change their lives. It wasn't a *bad* thing that he was born with no arms or legs. I'm sure he would tell you he would much rather have arms and legs, but if he had, he wouldn't be the person that he is. He has changed lives.

When you look at him, you gasp, thinking: *Oh my gosh! He has no arms and no legs!*

But then he talks, and you realize that he is brilliant. That man has such a heart; it changes the world. I can't say that if I had my leg cut off, I would be a happy person. I wouldn't; I would see that as a bad thing. But somehow that would motivate me. I wouldn't let that stop me from achieving my purpose or helping other people rise up.

I look at life in a positive frame of mind. Things happen. But clearly, events springboard me into helping lift up the rest of the universe as it ascends towards a heavenly existence.

Everything Always Works Out

Let's say my leg was cut off. Initially I would focus on losing my leg. I would mourn that I couldn't walk or run with my kids. There would be prosthetics to help me, but obviously I would prefer not to have my leg cut off. However, in the end, it would work out, because I will always continue on my path. I'm going to continue on my journey.

If you lose someone close, you perceive that as a horrible thing.

Why do you cry at someone's funeral?

Is it for them, or is it for you, because you're going to miss them?

They are likely now in the universal subconscious, able to feel the rhythm of the universe caressing their energy. They may not have the ego to be here, to give you their personality, or their conversation. But if you're going to cry, it better be because you're going to miss them, and you're crying for yourself. Don't cry for them, because they are free.

Everything will work out; it always does, as long as you're willing to push fear away. If you let fear guide your life, things may not work out, because fear is not of light. It's of darkness. Love what you want to do, and experience an absence of fear. All great things are coming to you. It will all work out in the end.

Things Will Be As They Will Be

You shouldn't worry. You should do your best at all times and not worry. Assume that regardless of what happens, God will make things happen as they should happen. Your only choice is to always do the best you can, and whatever will be, will be. That understanding can relax your mind enough to achieve all the great things you've ever wanted to achieve.

Let's say I want to open a functional medicine oasis, where people can fly in with all their chronic illnesses. I want to improve their health while they live on my property, a huge reserve of acreage. The program would take care of all the meal planning, the meals, the supplementation, and offer services from a variety of doctors and practitioners.

It would be a big investment and a scary thing to try because if people don't come, I would lose my entire life savings. The truth is, I *would* like to do that. It sounds like an amazing thing to do, and the only thing stopping me is fear. At some point, I will need to do that—obviously the plans will have to be worked out— because that's what I think the world needs. Things will be as they will be. So I can try, and if it doesn't work out, fine. God will guide me towards my next heaven.

You may think that your dream is to play music in a band. But along the way, the band doesn't work out and you find that, actually, you prefer to work fixing guitars, or work on the sound part of the music. Things will be as they will be. There's no reason to ever worry. You're always going to end up in your best heaven, as long as you're willing to take the steps necessary to try to become everything great that you've ever wanted to be.

ALL THINGS ARE ATTAINABLE

You should never leave your house scared if you are headed toward something you want. Understand that your life is a gift and that everything is attainable. If you don't grasp that nothing bad is going to happen to you, that everything is attainable, then you may not reach for what you want. If you don't reach for it, you've just wasted a portion of your life. When I say everything, I mean everything you could ever dream of, everything that you want. You say that you tried before and didn't get what you wanted. Well, everything that you *really* want is attainable. Maybe you thought one thing was your dream or goal, but it wasn't; your dream was something else.

You need to open your mind to the fact that sometimes God's plan for you is different than you realize. Although you thought one thing was your goal, the truth is, wherever you end up—as long as you're trying your best—is exactly where you are supposed to be. That place will give you more happiness than what you wanted in the first place.

What You Want Is Okay

What you want is okay. Never feel bad about being superficial or wanting something that you feel is shallow. It's okay to want to have a certain hairstyle.

It's okay to want to dress in certain clothes. You should be happy with what you have, but it's okay to have dreams and goals that include what you love or what you look for in a mate. There's nothing wrong with you. If you take care of yourself and live a life without fear, then you don't need to feel bad about anything.

You are who you are. Your soul wants this. Give to yourself what you want, without apologizing for it. So many people are worried to say what they want. I could say I want world peace. Great! World peace is a good thing. Maybe, what I really want is a nice car.

Is that a righteous dream?

Most people would say no, that wish is superficial; it's just a car. It's money. There's nothing wrong with wanting nice things. Nothing.

Obviously world peace is more important than having a nice car. Having food on the table is more important than having a nice car. Having a wonderful marriage, wonderful kids, and happiness is more important. Clearly there is a pyramid of needs here, but don't feel bad that you want something nice. Don't feel bad that you want to wear a specific hairstyle, or you want a special kind of makeup, or you want the new fragrance of perfume or cologne. There's nothing wrong with that. Take what you want, work for it, do great things. Don't ever apologize for what you want in life, even if other people deem it superficial. It is still righteous because it gives you fun in your playground of life, which is now.

Effort Will Be Required

Getting what you want is going to require energy. It's going to require effort. If everything was just given to you, and you didn't have to work for anything, nothing would have value. Instead of living in a heavenly existence, it would be a hellish one. Knowing that you need to work for certain things gives them value. Value is created by work or by the ladder of value we assign to things.

Certain brands of clothing are supposed to be very nice and very expensive, other brands of clothing are less expensive and less nice. There is a difference. Whether you're into nice clothing or not, giving a gift of a high-end, expensive shirt causes the receiver to probably value it more, knowing that it took more energy and effort to attain it.

If you want to be a great athlete it takes more than being strong and fast. You have to work to be the best. I don't know how many football players there are in the NFL right now, but all of them, *all* of them, put in effort. One of the best receivers of all time in football was Jerry Rice. He was not the fastest guy in the world, but he worked harder than practically everyone else.

Michael Jordan didn't make his high school basketball team, and now he's one of the best basketball players of all time. He kept working and working and working. It took effort, but he achieved his goal. It was attainable to him because he refused to give up. His energy and his effort overcame any type of solid, concrete foundation that would have stopped him from achieving his goals. He broke through walls by giving enough effort to break them.

If you want to be the best healer in the world, you must study more than everybody else. You will need to talk to people and care more than everybody else. You have to put in more time. Some people want to be successful, but they're not willing to put in the effort. You must prioritize working for your goal as higher than eating, or higher than going to sleep at night, or higher than spending time with your friends. Your primary goal has to be number one. If you put something as number one, you should be able to do it no matter what it is.

You Will Reach Your Goal

Your goal may not be clear to you right now, but if you work really, really hard, it will become clear. Let's say you think that your goal is to be a professional baseball player. You work hard at it, study the craft, and work out like crazy. In the end you may not be a baseball player professionally, but because you studied so hard you may end up being a coach. Maybe you would enjoy being a coach more than you would a baseball player, you just didn't realize it. It became clear later.

Your goals are absolutely attainable. If you realize you could never do it — remember the person with the terrible voice who wanted to be a singer — maybe that is not what will make you the most supremely happy. If you say you can't do something, therefore never try for it, that is failure. As a human, you have the ability to do anything you want, you just have to take the steps necessary to do so.

Look at the map. Look at what it's going to take to get there. Step by step, go through it. Figure out what it's going to take to get there. Work harder than everybody else, because if someone's working harder than you; they're going to get it and you're not. Hard work is necessary, and if you are willing to work hard, to give it your all, your whole spirit, you can achieve anything you want. You can attain what you want. It's all there, but you have to pursue it with love, passion, and a single-minded focus.

Nobody who is the best has gotten there by not trying. They all had a focus. Everything is attainable. You can achieve anything you want. Make a plan. Work hard at it. Sleep a little less. Get up a little earlier. Eat quicker. Go to work. Go do what you need to do to get there.

Chances are, you know what it takes to get there, and if you don't achieve it, it's because you weren't willing to do what it takes to achieve it. You chose not working for it as much as you needed to, rather than working hard enough to achieve it.

Conclusion

I hope that you now understand that all things are possible. I hope that this book inspires you to move forward in your life, and to achieve all the dreams and goals you've always had, but have been too scared to attempt.

Maybe you are sick. Maybe you have headaches all the time. Maybe you're tired. Maybe you don't have energy, libido, and maybe you don't look the way you want. Hopefully you have the courage and the energy to understand that your goals and your dreams are out there, attainable, and you can achieve whatever you want, as long as you're willing to take the first step to do so.

Understanding that everything is within your grasp should make this whole process easier. Have faith and get up every day determined. Make the decision that your goal is more important than lying in bed, more important than spending time with your friends, or going out for a cup of coffee. When you decide that you will achieve that goal no matter what, you take steps forward every day. You've created your plan; you're going to do it. Have faith that your work will be rewarded.

You have an opportunity now to achieve everything you've ever wanted. It's right in front of you. Imagine that you've already achieved it, because you have. You just need to go out and get it. You need to assume the reality already exists, lay yourself on that strip of consciousness, and take the steps necessary to achieve it.

Nothing bad is going to happen.

The question is will anything happen, or will great things happen?

That's up to you. You can choose to do nothing. Live your life the same way it was, act like you never read this book, act like this knowledge doesn't exist and none of it means anything. That is your choice.

But your other option, your other choice, is to live the rest of your life without fear, to know that we're all divinely inspired. You can achieve a healthy self and work toward taking care of your body so that your soul can find its way into this world. You can find the truth and achieve everything you need because you have the ability. You know the steps to take.

Go find yourself a natural health provider. Go find yourself an energy healer. Go find yourself a personal trainer. Go do whatever it takes to achieve and climb the ladder. Do whatever it takes to better yourself every single day, because although life is not linear and time doesn't really exist, growth does. Every day you have the option to grow. You also have the option to stay where you are.

Please, please, please make the decision to improve your life, because that will improve my life and everyone else's. It will improve your mom's and dad's, your sister's and brother's, your best friend's, your kid's, and your cousin's. We can spiral up the whole universe together. It is up to you to do so.

What I'd like you to do is make a plan today or tonight and write it down. Write down what you want. Write down the steps that you think it would take to get there. Be a little obsessive about it. Be detailed, and when you to go sleep tonight, have it in your mind that no matter what, you are starting to achieve your dreams tomorrow. Promise yourself to take the steps necessary to make your body healthy, your mind healthy, your soul healthy, and the angel healthy. Everyone can be happy, the rest of the universe can be happy, eternity can be happy, the whole corporeal world can spiral up with you, but it all starts with you.

There is a lot of pressure on you right now to make a decision, to change your life and the entire world. They are one. When you wake up tomorrow, I want you to check off the first thing on your list, the first thing you must do to achieve all your dreams. I want you to do it. Every day thereafter, I want you to wake up in the morning, and jump out of bed like a lion to serve your purpose.

You can do it. You know you can do it. It is possible. You wouldn't have the dream unless you were capable of achieving it. So if you wake up tomorrow and you do what you're supposed to do, you should congratulate yourself.

Look out in the world and say, "I'm coming!"

Because you are. You will achieve all the things that you've ever wanted to achieve. More than that, you'll help everyone you've ever loved achieve the things that they've wanted to achieve. You are going to inspire people. You're going to inspire everyone around you, and you can feel good about yourself every day.

What happens next?

You get to be happy. You get to be content, and you get to keep working toward goals, which are your purpose and dreams. You get to know that you will achieve them. All you have to do is keep taking the steps, one foot in front of the other. The path is in front of you. You will take it, and everything will work out.

Now, I'd like to give you a little gift to take with you. Start tomorrow with a good breakfast. Eat something for breakfast. Don't just get up and start your day. Eat something to fuel yourself. Create a spark within yourself, and make sure your breakfast feeds the body, which is carrying you to all your greatness. Make sure that you are having something that will nourish you, and not just taste good.

The nourishment is meant to help you get to your dream. The food that you eat is not meant to be your entertainment. The food that you eat should feed the life that entertains you. That entertainment that you receive should be realizing your dreams and feeding your being.

My gift to you is helping you understand that every-thing you do either takes you toward your dream, or keeps you where you are. It's now up to you to make the decision.

Will you make the plan?

Will you write in detail the steps you need to take?

Take your first step tomorrow, I don't care if there's some important thing tomorrow — someone's birthday or a trip out of town — it doesn't matter. You will take one step tomorrow, no matter what it is. You will take one step tomorrow toward your dreams and goals, because I want you to help lift *me* up. I want you to help lift the world up, and you can do that. The power is yours. I believe in you. Believe in yourself.

Thank you!

Next Steps

For video interviews with Dr. Goodbinder about many health issues please visit drgoodbinder.com.

About the Author

Dr. Jay Goodbinder grew up in Overland Park, Kansas, and moved to Lawrence to attend the University of Kansas to earn his undergraduate degree. There, he earned a Bachelor of Science in Education of Community Health. For his doctorate, he attended Cleveland Chiropractic College in Overland Park, Kansas, where he graduated valedictorian and magna cum laude. He became a member of Pi Tau Delta; joined the International Honors Society, was included in *Who's Who of All Colleges and Universities in the United States*, and received a prestigious research award for functional medicine therapies.

Dr. Goodbinder has several years of postgraduate education in functional endocrinology, functional biochemistry, and functional physiology and is now a board-certified chiropractic internist. He believes that everyone should be able to wake up every morning excited to fulfill their purpose in the world, and he is dedicated to making that a reality.

Made in the USA
Monee, IL
01 February 2021

58396843R00108